BRIDE'S BOOK
of
Traditions, Trivia & Curiosities

RACHEL CONARD
LISA WOJNA

BLUE
BIKE
BOOKS

The Publisher: Blue Bike Books
Website: www.bluebikebooks.com

Library and Archives Canada Cataloguing in Publication

Conard, Rachel, 1977–

Bride's book of traditions, trivia & curiosities / by Rachel Conard and Lisa Wojna.

ISBN 978-1-897278-51-2

1. Weddings—Miscellanea. 2. Weddings—History. 3. Marriage customs and rites. I. Wojna, Lisa, 1962– II. Title.

GT2665.C65 2009   395.2'2   C2008-905385-0

Project Director: Nicholle Carrière
Project Editor: Pat Price
Illustrator: Roger Garcia
Production: HR Media
Cover Image: Courtesy of Photos.com

We acknowledge the financial support of the Alberta Foundation for the Arts for our publishing program.

We acknowledge the financial support of the Government of Canada through the Book Publishing Industry Development Program for our publishing activities.

PC: 01

 Canadian Heritage   Patrimoine canadien

 Alberta Foundation for the Arts

DEDICATION

John, this book is dedicated to you. I loved every moment of our wedding day. Thank you for your constant love and support throughout my work on this book and throughout our lives. (Don't forget, you promised I can buy a plasma TV, now that this book is done!)

—Rachel Conard

To my parents, Mary and Mitchell Wojna. Through all the ups and downs life has pitched their way, they've still managed to celebrate 59 anniversaries. Here's to number 60. This one's for you both. Nasdrovia!

—Lisa Wojna

CONTENTS

ACKNOWLEDGMENTS

Thank you to the folks at Blue Bike Books for thinking of me and trusting me with this wonderful project. Many thanks also to our editor, Pat Price, for her hard work and assistance. And a special thank you to Lisa Wojna, my coauthor, who has been a dream to collaborate with. I hope to work with all of you again.

–Rachel Conard

As always, this project wouldn't be possible without the ongoing support of my family. Garry, Peter, Melissa, Matthew, Nathan, Jada and Seth—I love you all!

Any writer will attest to the fact that a great book is really a partnership. In this project, I not only had a wonderful coauthor—thank you, Rachel—I also had the privilege of working with a keen-eyed, sharp-witted editor, Pat Price. Thank you for all your hard work, Pat. To Nicholle Carrière and Blue Bike Books, who believed in this project and made it happen. And to my dear friend and mentor, Faye. Thanks, as always.

–Lisa Wojna

INTRODUCTION

In the course of my research for this book, it has been a real delight to immerse myself in all things weddings. I can think of no other occasion in which a single day (and the months and months building up to it) elicits so much joy, terror, surrealism, hysteria, contentment and alternating howls of laughter and throat-clenching tears. No wonder weddings are such a popular subject in film, as demonstrated by the numerous touching and funny wedding movie quotes sprinkled throughout this book.

We have come a long way from the days when the Anglo-Saxon term "wedlock" was literally translated as a "pledge of property." Cut to September 18, 2004. I'm waiting in the wings of my childhood church for an amazing, loving, funny man to marry me. I'll never forget my father opening the door to escort me. It was his first time seeing his youngest daughter in the white dress and veil, and he caught his breath and his knee buckled ever so slightly. (Forgive me, Dad, we all know you're a manly hunting-and-fishing kind of guy. You're allowed to be emotional at your daughter's wedding!) I don't know if he walked me down the aisle or if I was holding him up, but that walk remains one of my all-time-favorite father-daughter memories.

And I'll never forget John beaming at me as my father gave my hand to his. From the ceremony to the reception, my wedding day was as close to perfect as it could be. Which is not to say the event was completely devoid of drama. En route to pick up my fiancé and the groomsmen, the limo driver mistakenly went to the wrong hotel, an hour in the opposite direction! I was blissfully ignorant in the bridal chambers. My mother, however, was anything but blissful when the ceremony was only moments away and the groom had not yet arrived! Fortunately, a smooth-talking groomsman persuaded the hotel shuttle driver to transport them to the church. They arrived just in the nick of time!

With so many details to orchestrate and traditions to incorporate, few weddings are pulled off flawlessly. Yet, each has unique components and highlights that make it special, unable to be duplicated, an entity all its own, like a precious piece of time snipped from the line and encapsulated.

Like weddings, the tidbits, facts and anecdotes in this book are equal parts beautiful (an Iranian wedding custom of dotting honey into each other's mouths before the groom kisses the bride), funny (what not to say in a toast) and downright strange (um, Dennis Rodman in a wedding gown?). Whether you are planning a wedding, attending a wedding or just interested in history and trivia, you'll enjoy this light-hearted examination of wedding rituals both celebrated and endured when love joins two as one.

–Rachel Conard

Annie Banks: "What? What's that face?"

George Banks: "It's nothing."

Annie Banks: "Oh, this is going cost you more money."

George Banks: "No. It's just...I know I'll remember this moment for the rest of my life."

–Kimberly Williams and Steve Martin, *Father of the Bride* (1991)

THE PROPOSAL

At our most primitive, the idea of proposing marriage was nonexistent. If a man saw a woman he liked, he simply claimed her as his own and shipped her over to his house, where she lived out the rest of her years in his service. Of course, we are an evolutionary species, and that way of treating a lady didn't bode well for long. In England, for example, it was considered illegal for a man to steal his wife from her family by the sixth century—how advanced of those Brits! Asking permission to marry, from the lady in question and her father, became standard practice. And today, it's not uncommon for women to pop the question. We've come a long way, baby— where do we go from here?

Proof of Love

In some cultures, allowing a daughter to wed without the potential husband proving his worth to dear old Dad was unacceptable. These forward-thinking fathers demanded that their daughters' would-be suitors prove their devotion though hard, often-backbreaking labor. A prime example of this is the Old Testament story of Jacob and Rachel. Rachel's father demanded seven years of service from Jacob before he could enter wedded bliss with his beloved Rachel. Unfortunately, Rachel's father switched daughters before the vows were exchanged. Because it was tradition to cover the bride's head before the ceremony, Jacob did not know he had married the older daughter, Leah, until it was too late. A determined Jacob, broken-hearted but still intent on marrying his beloved Rachel, had to serve another seven years before he could marry his true love.

Examining the Situation

According to historian Shu Shu Costa, a serious matter such as marriage, which is responsible "for continuing the ancestral line and creating alliances between families, [is] too important a duty to be left in the rash hands of the young." So, in the Chinese tradition, the groom's parents pick out a potential mate for their son and appoint a middleman to approach the girl's family. Although technically an arranged marriage, this engagement has its own set of formalities before it's necessarily a done deal. The middleman, bearing gifts, meets with the girl's family and is charged with finding out the exact date and time of the girl's birth. This information, recorded on a formal document, is then put on a family altar for three days. Should anything occur during this time, from an extreme weather event to a family argument, which most certainly suggested a bad omen, the proposed union is called off. If the three days pass without any negative event, the groom's family takes the proposed union to the next step—an evaluation by an astrological expert, who examines the woman's birth date and time. If the numbers prove favorable, the groom's family sends word to the bride's family through the middleman and provides her family with their son's birth date and time.

The bride's family then goes through the same process. Even if both families come up with a good result, the marriage still isn't a sure thing. The families then meet and check out everything from the personal finances and social standing of their potential in-laws to their appearance and education. If the families pass muster against each other, the young couple is finally ready to enter into the betrothal stage. At this point, both families exchange traditional gifts of tea, bridal cakes and other symbolic items. The acceptance of these gifts means the bride and groom are betrothed. Although the betrothal is considered a formal and binding contract, it's quite likely the couple hasn't yet met. A year or two down the road, the two will finally be husband and wife.

Legally Binding

In Victorian England, a young man wanting to propose to his beloved first had to ask her father for permission. Once he received Dad's blessing, he could approach the girl of his dreams on bended knee and ask for her hand in marriage. At this time, however, British law viewed an engagement as a legal obligation. If the gent had a change of heart, it could get ugly—his former fiancée could sue him for "breach of promise."

Military Regulations

In many cultures, it is considered respectful for the man to ask the woman's father for permission to marry his daughter. For a Canadian military man, it is not only expected that he travel wherever necessary in the world to seek the bride's parents' personal approval, he also requires permission from his sergeant or superior.

Leap of Faith

Although it is customary for men to propose marriage, women in parts of the United Kingdom were gifted with one day every four years to exercise that privilege—February 29. Although details on the origins of this custom are far from clear, some sources trace the Leap Day proposal-switcheroo back to fifth-century Ireland, when St. Patrick began encouraging it after heated discussions on the matter with St. Bridget. Another story suggests the Leap Year proposal became Scottish law in 1288. And if the man declined? He was subject to a penalty, ranging from a kiss to buying the proposing lass a gift. Yet another theory proposes that, because February 29 was considered an anomaly and, therefore, exempt from the usual traditions and laws of the day, a single lady with her eye on a man could take advantage of the situation and ask for his hand in marriage.

By the Letter

In China, historically, the process of extending a proposal for an arranged marriage consisted of three formally written letters. First, the groom's family delivered a Request Letter to the bride's family to verify the arrangement of the marriage. Usually, this letter was accompanied by an initial gesture of gifts. When the groom's family subsequently sent more formal gifts to the bride's family, a Gift Letter was included. The Gift Letter, which often listed descriptions and quantities of the presents offered by the groom's family, was almost like an early form of a wedding registry. Lastly, a Wedding Letter was presented to the bride's family on the day of the wedding to finalize and confirm the marriage.

On Bended Knee

Although the exact origins of the bended-knee proposal are a little vague, historians and lay-folk alike theorize that royalty might have inspired the custom. It was common practice to go down on one or both knees to show respect for a king, queen or other person of power. And when a gentleman was knighted by his king or queen, he knelt to accept the honor. This act of supplication demonstrated humility, recognition of authority and surrender of oneself to another. When a man asked for a woman's hand in marriage, his bended-knee proposal represented the same things. By kneeling and bowing in humility and supplication, he was showing respect for the woman he loved. The action also symbolized praying—which makes perfect sense; the suitor was probably praying for the love of his life to accept!

Where's the Romance?

Today, only 60 percent of marriage proposals include a bended knee. Some men (about six percent) even propose to their girlfriends over the phone! (It is doubtful they are on one knee at the other end of the line.) At least it's better than texting a proposal....

DID YOU  KNOW?

According to a 2007 poll conducted by wedding website AisleDash.com, only 25 percent of women were "totally surprised" to receive a proposal. Call it women's intuition (or, in some cases, dropping major hints or ultimatums), but most women had an inkling the proposal was coming.

"Wood" You Marry Me?

Courting in Wales once included the suitor carving a wooden spoon and presenting it to his beloved. If she responded by wearing the spoon on a ribbon around her neck, she was considered to have accepted his marriage proposal. Now there's another romantic way to define "spooning."

A Clothes Encounter

In the North American Hopi Indian tradition, a young man with his eye on a particular lady proposed by leaving clothing at the door of her home. Her acceptance or rejection of the clothing signified a yea or nay to her suitor.

An Out-of-this-World Proposal

When a 29-year-old German man proposed to his girlfriend in June 2008, he accompanied the gesture by releasing 50 paper lanterns into the sky. His 27-year-old girlfriend said yes, and they enjoyed the romantic spectacle above. Unfortunately, their neighbors in the sleepy town of Plattling were not so entranced. Bavarian police received multiple phone calls from panicked people reporting strange lights and UFO activity!

The Best Marriage Proposal Is a Custom-made Proposal

Some marriage proposals are cliché: the ring in the dessert at the restaurant or at the bottom of a glass of champagne. If done right, they can still be romantic and more classic than cliché. But a proposal that is unique and tailored to the woman or the relationship is ideal. Take a lesson from this gentleman.

Graham McGowen was well aware of his girlfriend's affinity for snow globes. She was an avid collector, so when he decided to propose to her, he plotted for more than seven months to make it the ultimate global experience. On the anniversary of their first date, Graham took his love, Kristen, to their favorite park for a picnic and gave her a gift. She opened the present and discovered a snow globe. But not just any snow globe! Depicted inside was a woman sitting at a picnic table before a man on bended knee. The inscription on the plate read, "Will you marry me, Kristen?" She turned to Graham and found him exactly replicating the scene in the globe: kneeling before her at the picnic table, holding up a ring. She said yes. And when she shook the globe, glitter made from tiny diamond slivers showered upon the couple inside.

"*I guarantee there'll be tough times. I guarantee that at some point, one or both of us is going to want get out. But I also guarantee...if I don't ask you to be mine, I'll regret it for the rest of my life. Because I know in my heart...you're the only one for me.*"

–Maggie Carpenter (Julia Roberts) proposing, *Runaway Bride* (1999)

ROYAL PROPOSALS

When royal titles and merging families or even nations are at stake, one might imagine royal marriage proposals to be grandiose. However, many royal proposals are no different from those of any other giddy young couple in love.

Courting Elizabeth

Elizabeth Bowes-Lyon, who would eventually become known as Britain's Queen Elizabeth, The Queen Mother, was in no hurry to tread the road to royalty. She refused the future George VI at least four times in two years. Talk about playing hard to get! He finally wore her down on January 13, 1923, as they were taking a walk. When he asked again if she would marry him, to his surprise, she said yes. The long courtship was followed by a quick engagement period. They were married three months later, on April 26, and assumed the throne in 1936, when Edward VIII abdicated the throne.

Usurping the King

George VI's involvement—or lack thereof—made another marriage proposal less than smooth. Philip Mountbatten proposed to George VI's daughter, Princess Elizabeth, at Balmoral, the royal family's castle in Scotland, on a beautiful summer day. Elizabeth was thrilled and said yes! The faux pas? Philip had failed to ask the king's permission first. The young couple kept their engagement a secret for many months, and King George was furious when he finally learned of the arrangement. He felt his daughter, at the age of 20, was too young to marry. Nonetheless, in November 1947, the future Queen Elizabeth II married Prince Philip, the future Duke of Edinburgh, in London's Westminster Abbey with the King's eventual blessing. In 2007, the couple celebrated their 60th anniversary, along with about 2000 guests.

DID YOU  KNOW?

The engagement of Prince Charles to Lady Diana Spencer was not made public until three weeks after Charles proposed. The proposal occurred during a private dinner at Buckingham Palace on February 24, 1981.

Anything for Love

Edward VIII did not formally propose to American socialite Wallis Simpson on the quintessential bended knee. In 1936, he declared his intention to marry her by inviting Wallis to attend a formal dinner with him. His words were something along the lines of, "I would like my future Prime Minister to meet my future wife." Wallis was a bit taken aback, likely because she was still married to her second husband, Ernest Simpson. The scandalous affair between Edward and Wallis began in 1934, and, by 1937, Wallis had indeed divorced Ernest and married Edward. To claim his twice-divorced American bride, Edward was forced to surrender the throne, and the pair became known as the Duke and Duchess of Windsor.

When you make a sacrifice in marriage, you're sacrificing not to each other but to unity in a relationship.

–Joseph Campbell, American mythology scholar

PROPOSALS OF THE RICH AND FAMOUS

Who knew that politicians, musicians and even reality-TV stars could be so romantic? From simple and sincere to creative and extreme, famous people have proposed marriage in an interesting variety of ways.

My Funny Clementine

Sparks did not fly the first time Winston Churchill and Clementine Hozier met in 1904, but, when they were reintroduced in the spring of 1908, Winston went into overdrive in courting her. He proposed to Clementine on August 11, 1908, during a stroll through the gardens of Blenheim Palace. Clementine accepted, and a month later the two were married. As Winston himself once wrote, "I married and lived happily ever afterwards."

Childhood Sweethearts

Former Arkansas governor Mike Huckabee proposed to Janet, a girl he had known since junior high school, when both were just 18 years old. Unable to afford a ring at the time, he gave her a soda-can pull-tab. She said yes. Their vow to support each other in sickness and in health was tested just a couple of years later, when Janet was diagnosed with cancer of the spine. She pulled through just fine, and they will celebrate their 35th wedding anniversary in May 2009.

DID YOU KNOW?

On Valentine's Day 2005, Mike and Janet Huckabee upgraded to a covenant marriage, which limits their grounds for divorce. Causes for divorce in a covenant marriage are limited to abuse, adultery, abandonment or the commitment of a felony resulting in a prison term.

Sealing the Deal

To propose to German supermodel and *Project Runway* host
Heidi Klum, British singer Seal (birth name Seal Henry
Olusegun Olumide Adelo Samuel) took her to the resort
town of Whistler in British Columbia, Canada. There, on
December 23, 2004, in an igloo built just for the occasion on a
secluded glacier at an elevation of 14,000 feet (4200 meters), he
popped the question. Their relationship has been storybook ever
since. Other areas in which they score points for romanticism?
They married on a beautiful beach near Seal's villa in Puerto
Vallarta, Mexico. Accompanied by a Hungarian violinist, the
Grammy-winning performing artist serenaded his bride with a
song he wrote for the occasion. (The morning of the wedding
he was inspired to write another new song, called "Wedding
Day," which he later recorded as a duet with his new wife).
Once he and Heidi were pronounced husband and wife, Seal
got a "Kiss from His Rose."

Every May, Seal and Klum renew their vows before their friends and their growing family, which now includes children Henry Gunther Ademola Dashtu Samuel, Johan Riley Fyodor Taiwo Samuel and Helene "Leni" Klum (Klum's daughter from a previous relationship). For their most recent vow renewal in 2008, they revisited Mexico but added a decidedly Indian twist to the ceremony. Guests were instructed to dress in sherwanis and saris. The mostly traditional Indian ceremony was conducted by Shailesh Tripathi, a priest the couple met during a trip to India.

The Bad Boy Proposal

Although it was an unlikely match from the start, former New Edition singer and recent reality TV "star" Bobby Brown decided to take "every little step" closer to legitimizing his relationship with grand diva Whitney Houston. Despite their lavish lifestyle, he proposed with a surprisingly modest ring. Only after Houston said yes did he bust out the actual ring, an 11-plus-carat, emerald-cut diamond sparkler. Alas, after 14 tumultuous years of marriage, peppered with multiple arrests and trips to rehab, the couple called it quits for good.

Haunted Proposal

Two more reality-show alums (though, really, who isn't these days?), the stars of MTV's *Meet the Barkers*, shared a unique proposal. Was blink-182 drummer Travis Barker trying to scare Miss USA/Playboy Playmate/*Dancing with the Stars* contestant Shanna Moakler into saying yes—and not just by sporting enough tattoos and piercings to give small children nightmares? He bribed a ride operator at Disneyland to ensure some privacy when he got down on one knee in the Haunted Mansion and popped the question. The couple split after two years. Despite throwing herself a huge Las Vegas "divorce party," Moakler evidently still carried a torch. When Barker began dating Paris Hilton, Moakler's claws came out, and an altercation with the heiress resulted in the cops being called. Then, in September 2008, Barker survived a plane crash that tragically killed four others on board. He was hospitalized for severe burns, and Moakler rushed to his side. As of press time, those two crazy lovebirds have declined to confirm whether their relationship is on or off.

DID YOU  KNOW?

During his reign as piano king, the rhinestone-studded, ebony-and-ivory-tinkling Liberace received as many as 12 marriage proposals a week. Although he had many relationships and live-in partnerships with members of both sexes, and despite once admitting that he nearly married his actress friend Joanne Rio, Liberace never officially tied the knot.

Marry this Misfit—or Not

Look up "persistence" in the dictionary and you'll find a picture of British actor Rhys Ifans. The bloke best known for playing Hugh Grant's quirky, T-shirt-wearing roommate in *Notting Hill* first proposed to then-girlfriend Sienna Miller by scribing a Welsh poem that begged her to "Marry this Misfit." She said no. He then hid a ring in a pile of presents and proposed on her birthday. She said no. Undeterred, in his most elaborate scheme yet, Ifans created a code and hid clues on the bottoms of bottles of Miller's beauty products. Miller deciphered the code. Though, by now, did she really have to work very hard to figure out that he was proposing again? His intentions were pretty clear. But it worked. She finally said yes! Things have reportedly since cooled off between Ifans and Miller, though you can't say he didn't try.

When you meet someone who can cook and do housework— don't hesitate a minute—marry him.

–Anonymous

THE PUBLIC PROPOSAL

If there's one cliché to avoid, it's proposing via the JumboTron or a handmade sign pointed at the ESPN camera at a sporting event. For one thing, you risk very public rejection. Many have seen the YouTube video, first reported on a Fox Sports news segment, about the poor guy who proposed to his girl in the middle of the basketball court during halftime at a Washington Wizards game. Her reaction? She ran away faster than Gilbert Arenas with a fast-break dunk-shot opportunity! The young man was left holding the ring, the microphone and only a shred of dignity. However, for a lucky few, the public proposal works.

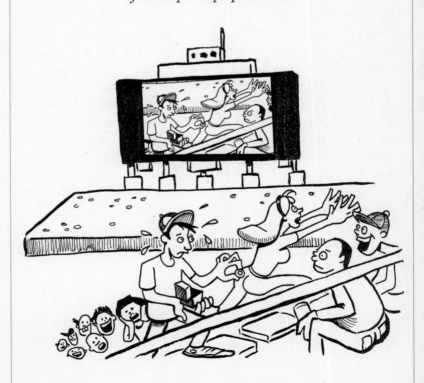

Country Lovin'

Country music superstar Garth Brooks proposed to Trisha Yearwood in front of 7000 fans during the Legends in Bronze Awards. As his statue was unveiled, Brooks got down on one knee and proposed. Yearwood accepted!

Lucky (and) in Love

In a 2007 episode of *The Price is Right*, contestant Rosie wore a red T-shirt with black lettering that spelled out "2399 Miles Three Times To Meet Bob." Naturally, she was referring to game show host Bob Barker. What she didn't know was that a glimpse of Barker would not be the only highlight of her trip. Her boyfriend Michael, sporting the same T-shirt, made it to the showcase showdown spin-off. As Rosie watched from the audience, Michael gave the wheel a hearty spin. Bob, in on the plan, immediately offered Michael the microphone, and Michael asked, "Rosie, will you marry me?" He held up a ring. The Big Wheel whirled fiercely in the background—perhaps Rosie was waiting to see how he did before replying—then, to the crowd's glee, landed on $1.00, meaning Michael had won $1000 and a place in the showcase showdown! Bob called out for Rosie to give the now-$1000-richer Michael an answer. Knowing a no-brainer when she saw one, Rosie cried out "Yes! Yes!" Cut to the showcase showdown, in which Michael emerged the big winner, taking home prizes worth $23,750. Rosie "came on down," and he slipped the ring on her finger.

DID YOU  KNOW?

The average engagement period in the United States is
16.5 months. The longest engagement on record belongs to
Adriana Martinez and Octavio Guillen. They became engaged
in Mexico in 1902 and finally married 67 years later, when they
were both 82.

Lights, Camera, Proposal

In March 2000, actress Angie Harmon had no idea her guest
appearance on *The Tonight Show* would be in any way unusual. To
her shock, boyfriend and NFL player Jason Sehorn walked onto
the set with a ring and proposed in front of the live studio audience and television cameras. Thank goodness Harmon said yes!

A man without a wife is like a vase without flowers.

–African proverb

ARRANGED MARRIAGES

In the beginning, according to Judeo-Christian belief, there was no world as we know it. And then God decided to change all that by creating a habitable planet and filling it with life forms of all kinds, including human. With the creation of Adam and then Eve, the Judeo-Christian culture was introduced to its first arranged marriage. It became the standard by which families participating in those faiths went about uniting sons and daughters in wedlock throughout history—and, in some instances, to this day.

Many cultures have specific belief systems surrounding arranged marriage, and, though some of the reasoning might differ from culture to culture and religion to religion, many of the factors considered in choosing a prospective spouse are similar: the candidate should be from a reputable family, be a member of the same or better social status, hold down a good job, preferably have a fairly flush bank account and share the same religious beliefs.

Never Too Young to Be Engaged

Back in the days when arranged marriages were the norm in China, a family's search for the perfect mate for their son was a complex process. If the groom's family was wealthy, the bride needed to be of equal stature and, most importantly, of strong fertility, to ensure that she would bear sons to inherit the family riches. Poor families sought hard-working brides. These matches were often determined when the couple-to-be was quite young, sometimes even before birth!

You May Now Meet the Bride

Marriages in the Muslim faith were traditionally arranged when the prospective spouses were about 10 years old. Although it rarely happened, girls could refuse to marry their betrothed. If the couple indeed married, it wasn't unusual for the bride and groom to meet for the first time on their wedding day.

Sealed with a Sip

Lobola is the complicated negotiation procedure that was customary for arranging marriages in Africa, and it is often still practiced today. Through formal written correspondence, the potential groom's family negotiated with the potential bride's family a price for the bride—historically, this usually meant a certain number of cattle. Although tension could escalate throughout the process, when terms were presumably agreed upon, the two families met. A bottle of brandy placed on the table, a gesture known as *mvulamlomo*, meant a deal had been struck. More than just a simple business transaction, lobola was viewed as a means for the two families to bond over compromise and mutual understanding. By the way, the bride and groom had no say in the process. They were usually forbidden to see each other until the wedding.

A Hairy Situation

When the Gilbertese, of the South Pacific Gilbert Islands, wanted to determine if a male was ready for marriage, they checked out his physical development. The benchmark? More than mere muscle mass, it was the growth of auxiliary and pectoral hair. Only when a young man displayed a prominent amount of hair was he considered ripe to marry. For some less-hirsute specimens, this was sometimes not until they reached their mid-twenties. Once established as sufficiently hairy, the men endured three years of education and training before earning the title of *rorobuaka*, or warrior, and being deemed fit to take a wife. For her part, when a Gilbertese girl began menstruating, usually in her early teens, she was confined to a *ko*, or "bleaching house," for about two years of preparation before being released for marriage.

Matchmaker, Matchmaker

In Korea, families traditionally brought their offspring's "résumés" to a professional matchmaker, who was enlisted to find a suitable mate. Because of the relatively low number of Korean surnames (about 300), it was important that families maintain meticulous lineage records, to avoid cases of mistaken identity or having distant relatives accidentally marry. Korean women traditionally do not assume their husband's name after marriage.

DID YOU  KNOW?

Although human resources departments generally discourage intra-office dating, each year, about 10,000 couples who meet or spark their romance during a coffee break at work eventually marry. So go ahead, single ladies, discuss last week's episode of *Lost* at the water cooler.

"Whether our parents introduce us, or whether we meet in a club, what difference does it make?"

–Hemant Rai (Parvin Dabas), *Monsoon Wedding* (2001)

THE DOWRY

Like everything else in life, the methods and processes of earning a maiden's hand in marriage evolved through the centuries. In time, the dowry system, in which fathers provided a payment of money and/or goods to prospective husbands, was introduced in many cultures. The implication or, at the very least, the hope was that the better the dowry, the better the husband.

Vybava and Veno, the Slovak Dowry

Marriage was typically the ultimate dream of every young Slovakian girl, and she began preparing for the big day from a very young age. Tradition has it that, as soon as the girl could thread a needle, her mother and the other matriarchs of the village would help her stitch together all the items she would someday need to run a well-ordered home. Not only would she make household items, such as kitchen cloths and bed linens, she also sewed clothing for herself and for the children she was most certainly expected to produce. As these items were completed, they were placed in a large trunk, which served as the girl's hope chest, or *vybava*. Linens her mother and grandmother had collected throughout the years, along with other family heirlooms, were also placed in the trunk, and this formed the girl's dowry.

At some point in Slovakian history, families began participating in the Hungarian custom of parading the bride's vybava from the home of her youth through the village and into her new home. The trunk was open, putting all of the bride's handiwork on display for villagers to comment on her potential success or failure as a new wife. Talk about pressure!

New brides also came with a second dowry called a *veno*. This more formal dowry, given in many cultural traditions throughout history, included everything from property to livestock and money, and, although it was presented to her new family, it belonged exclusively to the bride, giving her some independent security. The bride's family did not present the veno until about the time of the couple's first anniversary or when the first child was born.

Hope for the Future

Exact details surrounding this tradition are vague at best, but one source suggests a bride's father was originally responsible for building his daughter's hope chest. Throughout her youth, she collected the items she would one day need as a housewife and placed them in the chest. She also collected personal items, such as clothes and lingerie, and her parents enhanced the chest's contents with her wedding dowry, which was usually in the form of money.

DID YOU KNOW?

Hope chests were a common tradition in many countries, especially in Victorian England. In France, the hope chest held the bride's trousseau. The word comes from the French word *trousse*, translated as "bundle." It is thought that, when a French bride accompanied her new husband to his home, she carried with her a small bundle of her belongings.

A Mother's Love

In Greek tradition, a mother is responsible for preparing her daughter's dowry. From the time a girl is born, her mother knits or crochets doilies and tablecloths, sews bed linens and collects kitchen and other household items, which she stores away for the future wedding. The girl's father is not without his own jobs, however. His duty is to provide his daughter with her first home.

Well Endowed

In Indian tradition, marriage is viewed as one of life's most important decisions, and, because divorce is not an accepted practice in that culture, the process of searching out a life mate for a child pretty much begins at birth, especially for a girl. The girl's parents are responsible for collecting an adequate dowry—which, in some cases, can amount to tens of thousands of dollars. Although presented to the groom, the dowry was really an insurance policy of sorts, during a time when women didn't work outside the home. The dowry ensured provisions for the young woman, should the husband meet with tragedy or death, leaving her to care for herself.

The sum which two married people owe to one another defies calculation. It is an infinite debt, which can only be discharged through all eternity.

–Johann Wolfgang von Goethe, German author

DON'T MESS WITH THE DRESS

A good chunk of the wedding budget, and a whole lot of energy, goes into finding the perfect wedding dress. Even a frugal bride with a mother who sews is going to spend at least a few hundred dollars whipping up something special. And if the budget's slim and a used garment is the only thing available? No worries. Imagination, sprinkled with a few new ribbons and bows, can make a secondhand frock look like a million bucks. Whether it's money or time that's required, finding the right dress is all about turning the future "Mrs." into a princess for a day.

A Dress to Di For

When Lady Diana Spencer floated down the red-carpeted aisle of St. Paul's Cathedral to join her prince and become Princess Diana that fated July 29, 1981, little girls everywhere dreamed they, too, would someday become a vision in ivory, just like Diana. Although the royal marriage would not have a happily-ever-after fairytale ending, the dress Diana wore influenced brides and designers the world over for years to come. In fact, her wedding gown was so memorable that it inspired a book, *A Dress for Diana*, written by the dress's designers, David and Elizabeth Emanuel. Made of ivory taffeta and antique lace, the Emmanuel design sported a high neckline and a 25-foot (7.5-meter) train.

What 99.9 Percent of Us Are Wearing

Although, historically, royalty of all cultures routinely went all out when it came to purchasing the best cloth and creating the most elaborate dress for the big day, non-royals had to settle for what they had on hand. In the days before elaborate weddings and designer wedding gowns became the norm, a working-class bride traditionally used the best dress in her closet for her wedding gown, perhaps adding a new ribbon or two.

Ladies in Red

The traditional wedding dress in northern China, the *qipao,* is red in color. In Chinese culture, red represents strength and good luck and is believed to ward off evil spirits. Pakistani brides also wear red on their wedding day. In Pakistan, red symbolizes happiness and vibrancy. Because no one else is allowed to wear red to a wedding, the bright dress ensures that the bride is the center of attention. In India, white is considered a color for mourning, so wedding dresses are also traditionally red. An Indian bride has three style choices for her wedding dress: the sari, one large piece of cloth wrapped and pinned in place; the *gaghra choli,* a two-piece skirt and blouse set accessorized by a *dupatta,* or scarf; or a *shalwar kameez,* a two-piece pants and tunic set, also accessorized by a dupatta.

Well Wrapped

Korean bridal wedding garb includes a long-sleeved jacket, called a *chogori*, with two long ribbons tied to form the *otkorum*, or bow. A full-length, high-waisted wraparound skirt called a *chima* completes the ensemble. The bride also wears white cotton socks and boat-shaped shoes made of silk.

Stitching a Story

Intricate and colorful cross-stitch patterns, known as *vyshyvka*, typically cover the full blouse and skirt worn by Ukrainian brides. Originally, the cross-stitched patterns told a story, and each town or area of the country had its own traditional patterns.

Celtic Knot

A Celtic wedding dress is typically long and flowing, often sporting sleeves that gather at the top but hang loose and bell-shaped near the wrists. More traditional gowns might also have a front- or back-laced bodice, and it is quite common for a long, silk ribbon to trail from the waist down the length of the dress. A Celtic knot (symbolizing love eternal) is usually incorporated somewhere in the design, whether it is stitched onto the material or into a satin ribbon adorning the gown. As for color—there appear to be no taboos when it comes to choosing something more vibrant than white. It is not uncommon for brides to recapture their Celtic roots by choosing gowns of blue, green or royal purple over white or ivory for the special day.

The Bride Wore Shiro-maku

The traditional Japanese bride wears a white kimono, called a *shiro-maku* (which, translated, means white-pure). But this is not the only dress she will wear on her wedding day. The shiro-maku is worn only for the ceremony itself; for the reception, the bride adds a patterned silk kimono, called a *uchikake*, over top. Throughout the festivities, the bride can change her dress several times. The tradition originated in the 14th century and, according to one company specializing in traditional Japanese weddings, "signifies that she is prepared to return to everyday life."

DID YOU  **KNOW?**

Initially, wedding dresses mirrored the styles of the times, but in the 1920s, when hemlines started to rise, brides decidedly preferred the traditional floor-length gown for their special day.

The best and most beautiful things in the world cannot be seen or even touched. They must be felt with the heart.

–Helen Keller

THE COLOR SAYS IT ALL?

When we think of a wedding dress, most of us in North America think of a long, flowing gown in white or ivory. But where did the tradition of wearing a white wedding gown come from, and why do different cultures sometimes prefer different colors? When it comes to the meaning behind specific dress colors, theories abound.

A Change in Tradition

It was Queen Victoria who kicked off the tradition of wearing a white wedding dress. She rejected the then-traditional royal silver in favor of donning a gown of white satin when she joined Prince Albert in matrimony on February 10, 1840. After Queen Victoria's wedding, everyone wanted to get married in white— even if it was just in a nice, white housedress!

True Blue

Blue was the traditional color of wedding dresses in medieval England. Blue represented purity, and, if a bride could not afford a new blue dress for her special day, she usually included a hint of blue somewhere on her outfit.

DID YOU KNOW?

It was Spanish custom for the bride to wear a black silk dress, as well as a black lace veil.

White is Right

Cultural traditions aside, at least one superstitious rhyme of unknown origin makes predictions based on the bride's dress color. Black apparently inspires regret, as does red—the bride will "wish herself dead." Blue is, of course, true, but marry in green and you'll be "ashamed to be seen"—unless, of course, you're Irish. Then a green dress is a fine choice! Yellow is typically a cowardly color—a bride "married in yellow [is] ashamed of the fellow." Brown takes the bride out of town (and into the company of country folk), whereas gray transports the newly married farther afield. Pink has the habit of sinking spirits, and a pearl-colored dress promises a whirlwind life. White, simply put, is the right choice—at least, according to the poem.

DID YOU  KNOW?

Unless you were Irish, it was common knowledge that a bride wearing a green wedding dress should be "ashamed to be seen." A green gown suggested the bride was a tad promiscuous, having stained her dress by rolling about with her lover in the field.

Green in a Good Way

Not all weddings are white…you can also make yours green. And it doesn't have to mean you're promiscuous! How can the hybrid-driving, solar panel–housed couple have an eco-friendly wedding dress? A gently used dress is one option. Visiting a dressmaker who works with "green" materials is another. In the U.S., Olivia Luca uses fair-trade materials, and the United Kingdom's Wholly Jo can create a gown of organic cotton or hemp. No smoking the dress!

Black Monday

Always fashion-forward, *Sex and the City* star Sarah Jessica Parker wore black when she tied the knot to actor Matthew Broderick. Another unconventional choice? The ceremony was held on a Monday. Puts a decidedly upbeat spin on the term "Black Monday."

Wedding rings: the world's smallest handcuffs.

–Anonymous

UNUSUAL DRESSES

Most brides want their wedding dresses to be one-of-a-kind show-stoppers, but sometimes they can go overboard....

One Long Love Train

The longest wedding dress train on record—measuring more than 4468 feet (1362 meters) in length—was documented in 2007 in Cyprus. Green Leaf bridal shop designer Andreas Efstratiou created the clumsy bride's worst nightmare. One woman won a contest to model the piece. She strolled very slowly to live orchestral music, as 50 bridesmaids carried the train.

Made in Taiwan

Talk about sugar shock! In 1998, Taiwanese dressmaker Lu Sa-chou introduced one sweet creation. She designed and displayed a uniquely edible wedding gown made entirely of sugar. Comprising seven tiers of multicolored candy "flowers," the dress was even accompanied by a sugar veil, a sugar bouquet and sugar jewelry. The dessert took more than 250 hours to construct and weighed a whopping 44 pounds (20 kilograms). The groom might have a hard time carrying that bride over the threshold.

A Dress or a Mansion in the Hamptons?

The world's most expensive wedding dress was the product of a 2006 collaboration between Beverly Hills bridal salon owner Renee Strauss and jeweler Martin Katz. Featuring 150 carats of diamonds, the dress was valued at $12 million!

The Award for Most Hideous Wedding Dress Goes to...

Remember when heavily tattooed and pierced NBA bad boy Dennis Rodman showed up in a horse-drawn carriage at New York City's Rockefeller Center wearing a white wedding gown? Yeah, unfortunately, we can't forget either. Hard as we might try. It was a publicity stunt for his book signing at the Fifth Avenue Barnes and Noble bookstore. The book, aptly titled *Bad as I Wanna Be*, disappeared much faster than the disturbing image of Rodman in a wedding dress.

I have spread my dreams beneath your feet;
Tread softly because you tread on my dreams.

–W.B. Yeats, British poet

VEILS AND HEADDRESSES

The stories behind most traditions tend to be shrouded in ambiguity, and those explaining the origins of the wedding veil are no exception. One source suggests that, during the Victoria era, the veil symbolized a bride's purity and virginity. Another historian maintains the same meaning behind the use of the veil but dates its origins back to ancient Rome and Greece. In those days, veils were made of solid cloth and covered the bride from head to toe. Of course, covering one's face makes it a little difficult to walk gracefully down any aisle, and so it was that the father continued his role of protector, escorting his daughter and handing her over to her groom.

Lovely in Lace

George Washington's step-granddaughter, Nellie Custis, is credited with introducing the lace veil into society. She chose to wear a lace veil during her wedding ceremony to Lawrence Lewis on February 22, 1799, because it reminded the couple of an earlier meeting, when Lawrence saw his bride-to-be through lace curtains and thought her the most beautiful of maidens. When it came to innovation and forward thinking, apparently that apple didn't fall far from the tree.

Evil Repellant

For the Greeks, the veil (usually made from bright yellow or red cloth) was the most important piece of bridal clothing. Some sources suggest the veil symbolized the bride's virginity; others suggest that its purpose was to protect her from any evil spirits lurking about. The bride was not "unveiled" until formally handed over to the groom.

I Veil Myself

A Roman wedding ceremony places a high value on the wedding veil, which is traditionally red in color. It was the ancient Romans who gave us the term "nuptials," which comes from the Roman word *nubo* and, translated, means "I veil myself." Underneath the veil, a bride of ancient Rome wore her hair divided into six sections, each wrapped and secured into a cone shape, giving her the appearance of having a head full of spikes! The purpose behind this prickly hairdo, formally known as the *tutulus*, was to prevent demons from living in her hair, thereby keeping her purity and virginity intact.

DID YOU  KNOW?

A traditional Celtic bride often forgoes the use of a veil in exchange for a wreath of fresh flowers—what better way to symbolize purity?

Burning the Past

In Switzerland, the bride customarily wears a headpiece, usually a crown or wreath, to symbolize maidenhood. After the "I do's" are exchanged, the headpiece is removed and burned. The faster it burns, the luckier the bride will be.

A Maiden's Headgear

Young maidens of Ukrainian extraction wore an elaborate headpiece to signify that they had reached a marriageable age. Each region of the country had its own way of dressing up the headpiece, which was usually decked out with ribbons and beads and shiny bits and pieces to chase away evil spirits. Whenever a young woman attended a public event, from the weekly church service to a family wedding, she was expected to wear her headpiece, effectively advertising her availability. Once she was snatched up, the bride's female friends and relatives gathered the night before the wedding to make her a crown of flowers to wear during the church service in place of the headpiece. At the reception, the flowers, along with the veil the bride also would have been wearing, were removed and replaced with a traditional head covering called a *babushka*—a triangular scarf tied under the chin.

Sharing the Joy

A bride takes the symbolism of purity beneath the veil to exaggerated lengths during a wedding held in the Ukrainian tradition. She not only dances with every unmarried woman at her reception, she also places a veil over their heads to symbolize their purity and hope for future wedding bliss.

What Imperfections?

In the Japanese tradition, the veil is replaced by a *tsuno kakushi*, an ornamental wedding hat that has changed in appearance throughout the centuries. Literally translated, tsuno kakushi means "to hide horns." The Japanese bride acknowledges her metaphorical "horns" or imperfections (such as jealousy or selfishness) and the need to banish these tendencies from life as a new wife. Another traditional Japanese headdress is the *wataboshi*. The bride wears this large hood-like head covering to hide her face from everyone but the groom.

The Great Cover-up

In the ancient Judaic culture, the veil was not lifted from the bride until the couple was alone together and ready to consummate the marriage. Anyone familiar with the Old Testament story of Jacob and Rachel (in which Jacob was duped into believing he was marrying Rachel, when he was actually marrying her sister, Leah) will understand why this practice has changed somewhat throughout history. In traditional Jewish weddings, the groom is responsible for veiling his bride just before the ceremony. This practice is called the *bedecken*.

Rosemary Wreath

The night before a Czech wedding, either the bride weaves herself a crown or wreath of rosemary, or her mother and friends will make one for her. The rosemary is said to represent "wisdom, love, loyalty and remembrance." The bride wears the crown on her wedding day. Today, baby's breath and miniature roses are often substituted for the rosemary.

Switching It Up A Little

One traditional Polish wedding tradition has the bride and groom making a few adjustments to their wardrobe. When she enters the reception hall, the bride's veil comes off and she dons a small, lace head covering called a *czypek*, which she wears throughout the remainder of the festivities. The switch in headgear symbolizes her move from the life of a maiden to that of a wife. The groom, too, dons a quirky, brightly colored hat (which symbolizes happiness and laughter). The couple is also adorned with a ribbon necklace decorated with miniature dolls (symbolizing lots of healthy children in the future).

Putting a Lid on It

At least one cultural tradition includes what is often referred to as a capping ceremony. In the Slovakian tradition, a simple marriage cap called a *cepec* replaces the elaborate maiden's headpiece or wreath. Usually, the bride's mother, godmother, grandmothers or some combination thereof work together to remove the headpiece, braid the bride's hair in a single, long plait and place the new cap on her head. Following the wedding, the bride is expected to wear the cepec whenever she is in public. A traditional Slovakian groom is adorned with a shepherd's hat after he says his "I do's."

DID YOU  KNOW?

Former U.S. President Teddy Roosevelt is credited with initiating the trend of grooms wearing tuxedos on their wedding day. Roosevelt was married twice—once in 1884 (sadly his first wife, Alice, died a few days after giving birth to the couple's first child) and then again in 1886. It is not clear if he donned a tuxedo for one or both weddings.

A happy marriage is a new beginning of life, a new starting point for happiness and usefulness.

–Dean Stanley, British theologian

SOMETHING BORROWED, SOMETHING BLUE

Something old, something new,
Something borrowed, something blue,
And a silver sixpence in her shoe.

Ever wonder where the rhyme "Something Old, Something New, Something Borrowed, Something Blue" came from? Although its origins are not entirely clear, some sources suggest the British rhyme began during Queen Victoria's reign. Theories differ as to the meaning behind these sage words, but here are a few interpretations.

Something Old

Some historians have theorized that the "something old" refers to the original family and friends the newly married couple had before they tied the knot. It is often represented by a piece of heirloom jewelry passed down to the bride by a family member on her wedding day. The hope is that these important premarriage relationships will continue to be important as a new family is being established. Alternatively, a bride can carry a lace handkerchief that has been passed down for generations. The hankie may come in handy—superstition has it that a bride who cries on her wedding day will never cry over her marriage!

Another version of the "something old" is the tradition of a married woman giving the bride her old garter. This signified a passing on of luck and happiness to the new bride.

Something New

The "something new" directive—which, given the fact that, at the very least, most brides purchase new lingerie for their wedding day—is not difficult to comply with. This new item symbolizes the new marriage and, in particular, the new role in life the bride is about to assume.

Something Borrowed

The "something borrowed" is also often provided by a family member. A bride might borrow a piece of jewelry, especially something passed down through the generations. Or the groom might borrow a buddy's car for the couple's post-reception getaway. Either way, the borrowed object must be returned to ensure that good luck follows.

Something Blue

Most sources appear to agree on the meaning behind "something blue." Because the Virgin Mary is often portrayed wearing blue, the color is said to symbolize purity and fidelity.

DID YOU KNOW?

Another dress-related tradition, hearkening back to the days when brides took great pains to meet the old, new, borrowed and blue criteria, is the practice of inserting a "silver sixpence in her shoe." The money supposedly ensures the new bride a wealthy future.

Two human loves make one divine.

–Elizabeth Barrett Browning, British poet

NAMING THE DAY

*Although some couples decide to tie the knot and then do it on
the first convenient date, in some cultures, choosing the right
day is an important part of planning a wedding.*

Of Astrological Significance

In the Chinese tradition, couples should only marry on "lucky
days," so the Chinese lunar calendar plays a large role in deter-
mining a couple's wedding day. Based on the positions of the
Sun and Moon in relation to the Earth, this very complicated
calendar determines which days are considered lucky. Because
the positions of the Sun, Moon and Earth change constantly,
those lucky days also change each year. Marry on one of these
lucky days, it's said, and the marriage will be a long, prosperous
and happy one.

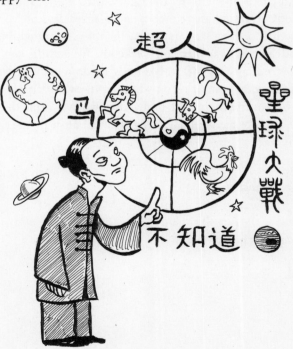

Food First

Because food is an important part of the wedding festivities in Greek culture, couples are not allowed to hold their wedding on a Christian holy day or fast day. The reasons for this are two-fold: the focus of a holy day should be on the Christian celebration; and how on earth can you enjoy a feast during a day of fasting?

Council Says

According to one source, lovebirds in the Mohawk tradition can marry at any time of the year, as long as the Council of Chiefs agrees on the date. When a couple decides to marry, they are expected to approach the Council of Chiefs on the matter.

Recipe for a Happy Marriage

When it comes to choosing the right day to marry, superstitions abound! Certain dates are taboo, and specific days of the week and months of the year carry a specific meaning. Weddings did not traditionally take place on weekends. In fact, the concept of the weekend, as we know it, is a fairly modern convention. Therefore, couples married on whatever day was deemed convenient. Of course, there were preferences when it came to choosing the appropriate weekday. An ancient English rhyme spells it out this way:

Marry on—
Monday for wealth,
Tuesday for health,
Wednesday, the best day of all;
Thursday for crosses,
Friday for losses,
Saturday, for no luck at all.

Notice a mention of marrying on Sunday is completely over-looked. That is because Sunday was considered a holy day, and, where Christian observances were held, the day was considered sacred and set aside for God.

The Right Month

Rhyme is also used to speculate on the best months of the year to marry. However, there is more than one rhyme on the topic, and their messages do not all agree. Here is one ancient English rendition:

Married when the year is new, he'll be loving, kind and true.
When February birds do mate, you may wed or dread your fate.
If you wed when March winds blow, joy and sorrow both you'll know.
Marry in April when you can, Joy for Maiden and for Man.
Marry in the month of May, and you'll surely rue the day.
Marry when June roses grow, over land and sea you'll go.
Those who in July do wed, must labour for their daily bread.
Whoever wed in August be, many a change is sure to see
Marry in September's shrine, your living will be rich and fine.
If in October you do marry, love will come but riches tarry.
If you wed in bleak November, only joys will come, remember.
When December snows fall fast, marry and true love will last.

In another version, marrying in January is not such a good thing—you are likely to be widowed "before your prime." Marry in March and you will likely move to some distant country. Marry in April and "a chequered path before you lies." A June wedding promises "one long honeymoon." And July is apparently a bittersweet month to marry.

Avoiding May

For centuries, couples avoided marrying in May because it was considered the most unlucky month in which to say your "I do's." This belief seems to stem from a number of sources. The Pagan festival of Beltane, with its bent toward forms of sexual expression, was held during that month, making it an unsuitable choice for such a solemn celebration. Two ancient Roman festivals—the Feast of the Dead and the Festival of Bona Dea, the "Good Goddess of Chastity"—were both held during May. Let's face it, celebrating death and a life of chastity does not bode well for a long marriage with lots of children!

According to Scottish lore, a firmly believed saying suggests, "Marry in May and your barns will decay." Horseshoes were kept on barn doors to ward off evil spirits, and even today, Scottish brides and grooms are given horseshoes for good luck.

The belief that May was an unsuitable month to marry was so strong, it was said that Queen Victoria, who reigned from 1837 to 1901, absolutely forbade her children to marry during that month!

June Bride: Cliché or Fact?

For today's couples, time and weather concerns tend to dictate the wedding month. With the exception of January, which is very unpopular (though likely not due to fear of premature widowing), the percentage of total weddings that take place in any given month is fairly evenly distributed throughout the year.

January: 4.7 percent

February: 7.0 percent

March: 6.1 percent

April: 7.4 percent

May: 9.8 percent

June: 10.8 percent

July: 9.8 percent

August: 10.2 percent

September: 9.6 percent

October: 9.4 percent

November: 7.4 percent

December: 7.8 percent

Picking the Date

Numerology plays a role in all kinds of superstitions. Both also play a role where marriage is concerned. It was nothing short of foolish for a bride and groom to marry on the same date as either of their birthdays—bad luck was sure to follow a couple making that faux pas! It was also considered bad luck to change your wedding date once it had been set. And at least one ancient custom offers prospective couples a list of the most beneficial dates throughout the year to marry. Of course, the list is really null and void if celebrations such as Lent happen to fall on any of the suggested dates. After all, one would have to be a fool not to adhere to a superstition that states: "Marry in Lent, live to repent."

Choosing the Hour

Superstition dictates that a couple should say their "I do's" during the day. To make your vows after dark invites darkness into the marriage—an early death for the bride, groom or any future children or the early death of the marriage through some other calamity, such as divorce.

Jackpot Wedding Day

Whether it was chosen for good luck or because it was an easy date to remember, July 7, 2007 was the date of choice for a host of weddings. For Vegas regulars, the 7/7/07 wedding date comprised the jackpot number of three 7s—a slot machine winner and a winning hand (21) in blackjack. NBA star Tony Parker and actress Eva Longoria decided to try their luck and tied the knot that day, as did celebrity chef Wolfgang Puck and his long-time love, handbag designer Gelila Assefa. Other venues got in on the once-in-a-millennium date. The Phoenix Zoo was the site of no less than 77 weddings on that date. And theme park giant Six Flags handpicked seven couples to marry on their favorite rides at 7:00 AM on 7/7/07. In related news, a posse of potheads were stoked to get married on 4/20 but forgot to apply for marriage licenses.

"Love can't be perfect. Love is just love."

–Massimo (Justin Chambers), *The Wedding Planner* (2001)

WEDDING PLANNING TRENDS

From high-tech invitations in the latest hot colors to eco-aware receptions, here are some of the biggest trends cropping up in the wedding planning world.

Eco-friendly Wedding

People are going green, these days, and there's no reason you can't do the same on your big day. It is becoming increasingly popular for environmentally conscious couples to insist that all glass and plastic bottles from the reception be recycled. Other ideas for getting onboard with saving the planet:

- use hemp paper for the invitations;

- give seedlings or potted plants as party favors;

- book a green venue, such as the Lady Bird Johnson Wildflower Center in Austin, which will gladly furnish your event with environmentally friendly LED lights and food from local farmer's markets;

- donate superfluous food to a homeless shelter or food bank—you can even claim a tax deduction for the donation.

Save a little money, plus help make the planet healthier for your children and grandchildren to come.

DID YOU KNOW?

Pantone, Inc., the world-renowned authority on color, chose Pantone 18-3943 Blue Iris as its 2008 Color of the Year. The company described the bluish-purple tone as "a multifaceted hue reflecting the complexity of the world that surrounds us." Its popularity has been reflected in current wedding invitation trends.

You are Cordially Invited...

Here are the top ten modern invitation trends, provided by the wedding-invitation experts at mygatsby.com.

10. The color blue—along with blue iris, picture Tiffany-blue, aqua and navy.

9. Super girly—think frills, lace and ultra-feminine.

8. Earthy—colors and images inspired by nature are hot; think birds, trees, flowers and representations of the four elements: sky, earth, fire and water.

7. Gray: the new black—'nuff said.

6. Creative shapes—come late spring, people are inundated with wedding invitations; circle, octagon, triangle and heart shapes stand out.

5. Flower patterns—see trends 8 and 9.

4. Unusual fonts—anything goes when it comes to type styles and even font colors.

3. A touch of yellow—bright yellow accents are the rage, and brides often include a coordinating peek of canary color in their wedding flowers or sashes for the bridesmaids.

2. High-tech—paper invitations are a given, but going with the hot blue-iris color and gunmetal gray type gives them an edgy feel; to make them even more modern, include your wedding website info or a CD or DVD of wedding information.

1. BOLD—no more demure brides; invitations are increasingly splashy and statement-making.

DID YOU KNOW?

The average number of guests invited to a wedding is 175. The largest documented wedding ever attended was in Jerusalem in 1993; about 30,000 guests attended the Jewish service!

All But a Ghost Town Except for the Brides

All that remains of the town of Bridal Veil in the Columbia Gorge in Oregon is a post office, a church and a cemetery, but it refuses to become a ghost town. Each year, thousands of brides visit the town to drop off their wedding invitations at the post office to have them stamped with the Bridal Veil postmark.

"I used to think a wedding was a simple affair. Boy and girl meet, they fall in love, he buys a ring, she buys a dress, they say I do...I was wrong. That's getting married. A wedding is an entirely different proposition."

–George Banks (Steve Martin), *Father of the Bride* (1991)

GIFTS AND GATHERINGS

Everybody loves a party, and what better reason to celebrate than a wedding. A bridal shower or three is a must, especially if the Mrs.-to-be hasn't lived the swinging bachelorette lifestyle and needs a little help setting up house. And we can't leave the groom out, so you know what that means...a night out with the boys!

The Bridal Shower

The custom of throwing a bridal shower—a gathering of the bride's friends and family to celebrate the coming wedding and "shower" the guest of honor with gifts for her new home—is said to have been inspired by a legend that dates back to the Middle Ages. The story tells of a forbidden love between the daughter of a wealthy man and a poor village miller. When the couple married against the father's wishes, the daughter was disinherited. Without even the benefit of a traditional dowry to draw upon, the couple was left with no means of setting up a home. Although poor, the miller was a well-respected member of the community, and, on hearing of the couple's plight, the miller's neighbors got together and "showered" the new bride with household items. The modern-day bridal shower is an early 20th-century American invention started by women of high society.

Open Carefully

It's believed that, as the bride-to-be opens her shower gifts, each broken ribbon signifies a child the marriage will produce. Some brides save the ribbons and create a faux bouquet to be used at the wedding rehearsal. There goes that tradition.... These days, presents are often given in gift bags.

The Bachelor Party

The traditional bachelor party's origins hearken back a little farther than the bridal shower's, into ancient Sparta. Sometime around the fifth century BC, soldiers started hosting a feast for their buddies on the night before the wedding. The feast was a way of sending the groom-to-be off with their very best wishes and providing him with a last night out before settling down to a life of domesticity. Of course, when you've got a good thing going, you don't want to give it up it without good reason—the bachelor party tradition spread to neighboring cultures and has continued to be a key part of pre-wedding festivities ever since!

DID YOU  KNOW?

Although it might be called a bachelor party in the United States, the last night as a swinging single for the groom is referred to by a few other names in other countries: in South Africa, it is often called a bull's party; in the United Kingdom, Ireland, New Zealand and Canada, that last night of freedom is called a stag party or stag night; and Aussies call the bachelor party a buck's party or buck's night.

Radical Registry

Lorelei Sharkey and Joey Cavella didn't just ensure that their unique, nontraditional wedding would be talked about for months to come; their gift registry generated a few opinions, as well. According to an article in *Modern Bride*, the couple set up a PayPal account, so friends could donate money for an Italian honeymoon. Sharkey told reporter Laurie Sandell that this was the only way she and her new husband could take the honeymoon of their dreams!

Realistic Registry

With couples opting to tie the knot later in life, gift registries are becoming less about the necessities of daily living and more about what's *really* needed. Face it, likely the bride and groom were either set up in their own apartments or already living together, and the day-to-day necessities, such as dishes and silverware, were purchased long ago. Couples looking to the future are registering at home renovation centers and asking for things such as drywall and paint for their new house.

Furnishing Party

A Moroccan pre-wedding tradition is the Furnishing Party. As the name suggests, this tradition involves furnishing the bride's new home. The party, which takes place exactly five days before the wedding, is usually attended by the women in the bride's life, who deliver everything from carpets and a mattress to handmade blankets and linens.

> Jane: *"Wanna go find the ugliest stuff in the store and register Tess for it?"*
>
> Kevin: *"Let's do it."*
>
> –Jane Nichols (Katherine Heigl) and Kevin Doyle (James Marsden), *27 Dresses* (2008)

WEDDING TRADITIONS AROUND THE WORLD

If you've been to a few weddings in your day, you'll know that each wedding is as unique as the couple getting married. Although everyone is interested in the latest fads, ethnic and cultural traditions often play a large role in the couple's final planning decisions.

Father of the Bribe

Prior to the 1940s, traditional wedding plans in Bulgaria began long before the wedding day. When a man of marriageable age was ready to propose to his sweetheart, he had to approach her and her father through a series of specific steps. First, he would gather a bottle of homemade brandy (*rakia*), a bouquet of zdravets flowers (for health and prosperity), and a couple of small gift items for both his planned bride-to-be and her father. The young man then packaged up all these items and had a few of his best buddies approach the girl and her father. This meeting was called a *sgleda*. The young man's intentions were presented to the father and, if he approved of the gentleman in question, he asked his daughter three times if she wanted the marriage. Once she confirmed that she was indeed ready for this big life commitment, her family sent the young men off with a few gifts for the would-be groom.

As lavish as all this might seem, the engagement was not made official until an engagement party, complete with a huge feast and lots of libations, was held at the bride-to-be's family home. During this feast, which was usually held on a Sunday or a special holiday, wedding plans and responsibilities were hashed out between the couple's families, and a wedding date, usually a year or more down the road, was set.

Please Eat the Invitations

Weeks before a Czech wedding, the bride and her helpers gather to bake *kolache*—small pastries stuffed with cheese or fruit fillings. The kolache are handed out to friends and family as formal invitations to the upcoming wedding and reception.

The Grinding Girl

A unique Iranian tradition is that of the "grinding girl." The night before their wedding, the bride and groom sit together with four of their unmarried women friends. While these women hold a white cloth over the bride and groom's head, a woman of impeccable honor, chosen by the bride's and groom's families, begins grinding two nuggets of sugar together. As she does this, she prays that God will protect the couple from all evil spirits.

Setting the Bar

Families in the Czech Republic have a unique way of finding out what kind of husband or wife their offspring will marry. When a father wants to check out the qualities of his future son-in-law, he places an axe and chopping block and a bottle of wine by the front door of the bride's family home. If the young man picks up the axe, it is said that he will be a "good house-man." Go for the wine, however, and it is a sure sign he will be a no-good drunk someday.

The future bride is similarly tested the first time she walks through the door of her groom's family home. A broom is placed in plain sight, and, if the bride picks it up and gives the floor a good once-over, she will be a good housewife.

DID YOU  **KNOW?**

In some African communities, an imposter disguises herself as the bride during the engagement party, and the groom is charged with telling the difference!

Preparing Through Seclusion

The first major ceremony in a Pakistani wedding begins 8 to 15 days before the big day. This is when the bride enters *mayun*, a state of seclusion in which she is purified and prepared for the wedding ceremony. Turmeric, sandalwood and assorted herbs and oils are blended to form a paste called the *uptan*. After the groom's mother and sisters bless the bride, they apply the paste to the bride's face and hands. This paste is repeatedly massaged into her skin each day leading up to the wedding, and it remains on for most of every day. The bride must stay in seclusion during this entire time and will not see the groom again until she is presented to him at the wedding ceremony.

In some circles, the groom goes through a similar ritual with his bride's mother and sisters. The groom has a little tougher go of it, however—his bride's relatives often use this time to tease their soon-to-be new family member.

The Fattening Room

In Nigerian culture, the bride-to-be will sometimes spend time in a "fattening room." Here, she is taught how to be a good wife and (as the name suggests) is kept well fed! Before the ceremony, she is cleansed in a special bath, and her feet are again washed after the ceremony, so she is clean when she goes to her new husband.

Kind of a Ripoff Compared to the Fattening Room

South of Nigeria, in Namibia, the Himba people kidnap the bride the night before her wedding day and fit her with a leather marriage headdress. After the ceremony, she is anointed with butterfat from cows.

Lovey Dovey

In preparation for her wedding, a bride in the Philippines constructs a "cage" of flowers. Two white doves are put into the cage and then released after the wedding ceremony.

Pulling his Weight

Creeling is an old Scottish tradition in which the groom was tasked with hoisting a large basket (or creel) of stones on his back. He was forced to carry the creel from one end of the village to the other, until his intended bride came out of her house and offered him a kiss.

One should believe in marriage as in the immortality of the soul.

–Honoré de Balzac, French novelist and playwright

THE NIGHT BEFORE THE BIG DAY

In many cultures, planning a wedding involves a good deal more than sending out invitations and organizing a feast. Rituals taking place the night before the big day are common—and often as elaborate as the wedding-day preparations themselves.

The Cockloft and Bridal Bed

In China, the bride retreats to a cockloft the night before the wedding for a sleepover. (For clarity's sake, a cockloft refers to an isolated or separated place in the house, perhaps originally the family's barn.) But the bride is not alone. Her friends gather with her, singing songs criticizing her future in-laws—and even her own parents—for allowing this wedding, which will inevitably lead to the bride's separation from her birth family, to take place.

The groom's pre-wedding preparations are a little more practical. He is responsible for preparing his marriage bed. The day before the wedding, a "good luck" person—a man or woman with lots of children, assists the groom in putting the bed together. Before the new couple starts out their married life, children are invited to pile onto the bed for good luck. This, along with a scattering of dates and other fruits and the help of the "good luck" person, is believed to ensure the couple's fertility.

Ensuring a Good Hair Day

The night before the wedding, it was also an ancient Chinese custom for both the bride and groom to separately partake in a four-part hair-combing ritual.

- ☛ The first combing represented "from beginning till the end."

- ☛ The second was for "harmony from now till old age."

☛ The third combing was meant to bring an abundance of "sons and grandsons."

☛ The fourth combing symbolized "good wealth and a long-lasting marriage."

Just before the ceremony, the bride and the groom each partake in a cleansing bath, meant to wash away any negative energy. The bride's hair is dressed by a "good luck" woman, and the groom's father adorns his son's head with a cap overflowing with cypress leaves—another tradition bestowing good luck.

Elaborate Art

In India, the night before a traditional wedding is filled with symbolic activities, including henna. A ceremonial bath is prepared for the bride by her maternal aunt, who is then also charged with washing her feet. Following the bath, the bride's eldest auntie uses a henna stain to decorate her hands, feet and parts of her legs and arms with *mehendi* (also referred to as

mehndi)—elaborate tattoo-like designs. Some historians suggest that mehendi originated in the time of the pharaohs more than 5000 years ago and was later imported to India. Others believe it originated in India. Either way, the henna used in creating the bride's mehendi usually comes from the *Lawsonia inermis* bush. Unlike press-on tattoos, this body art lasts for several weeks—longer still, if you take care of it. This worked well for the bride, because, traditionally, she wasn't expected to do a stitch of housework until the henna was gone!

Today, although many modern Indian girls still like to have mehendi applied before their wedding day, the tradition has changed a little. Instead of an aunt, her girlfriends are likely to be the ones painting the design and, in the process, giving the bride a lot of advice for her wedding night!

DID YOU KNOW?

Long before it was popularized by Madonna, henna was used in the Middle East as a substitute for the lavish jewelry that only very wealthy Muslim brides wore.

Jeremy: "John? I need to see you right away. It's important."

John: "What's going on?"

Jeremy: "We got three big weeks ahead of us. It's wedding season, kid!"

–John Beckwith (Owen Wilson) and Jeremy Grey (Vince Vaughn),
Wedding Crashers (2005)

BIG LOVE: WHEN ONE IS NOT ENOUGH

The common dictionary definition of polygamy is "the practice or condition of having more than one spouse, esp. wife, at one time." Although the definition is pretty standard, different cultures throughout the ages have adapted the idea to fit their customs in many ways.

There are three basic forms of polygamy: polygyny (one man with many wives); polyandry (one woman with many husbands); and group or circle marriage (in which a number of women and men form the family group). Polygyny is the most common form of polygamy. Multiple marriage of any kind is not considered legal in the United States and Canada.

Theological Viewpoint

Christian theologians have argued through the ages that, although multiple marriage unions might have been acceptable and even necessary for the successful procreation of humanity in the beginning of life, as we know it, this has not been the case for some time now. Polygamy is not accepted in the Christian church proper, and the scriptural basis for this can be found in New Testament passages, such as 1 Timothy 3:2, "A bishop then must be blameless, the husband of one wife, vigilant, sober, of good behavior, given to hospitality, apt to teach."

Marital Revelations

Polygamy became an accepted practice in the Mormon Church, also known as the Church of Jesus Christ of Latter Day Saints, after founder Joseph Smith Jr. claimed he had received a revelation from God that some Mormon men could practice "plural marriage." The date of that revelation was July 17, 1831.

However, ongoing revelations led that church administration to adjust its views, and, in 1910, the church issued a new policy declaring plural marriage an unacceptable practice for people of the Mormon faith.

Traditional Views on Multiple Marriage

☛ Polygamy was banned throughout East Asia with the Marriage Act of 1953.

☛ Hong Kong only banned polygamy in 1971.

☛ Hindu marriage law prohibits the practice of polygamy in India for Hindus, Jains and Sikhs, but the civil legalities of the practice vary in different regions of India. Indian Muslims are allowed to have more than one wife.

☛ The practice of polygamy is not foreign to the Hebrews of the Old Testament. However, most Jewish sects have outlawed the practice. The State of Israel does, however, make exceptions for immigrant Jewish families who had entered into polygamous marriages in countries where the practice was accepted.

☛ Theravada Buddhists consider polygamy sinful, stating "a man who is not satisfied with one woman and seeks out other women is on the path to decline." Tibetan Buddhists, however, might entertain taking on a second companion for "spiritual practices," especially if the husband and wife are at different stages in their spiritual journeys.

☛ Although traditional Islamic law allows plural marriage, polygamy is not practiced by all followers of the Muslim faith, and some Muslim countries—Tunisia and Turkey, for example—have made the practice illegal.

One, Two, How Many Will Do?

In traditional Chinese culture, a man was allowed just one wife. The next woman to capture his heart was relegated to the position of concubine, or "little wife"—even if he preferred her to his wife. Although he could have as many concubines as he liked, a man was responsible for keeping his wife and his concubines in relative comfort. However, should his wife not conceive a child, and if she still had family to which he could return her, the husband could divorce his first wife and take another. That second wife might or might not be chosen from his several concubines. In 1949, with the establishment of the People's Republic of China, Chinese law restricted marriage to one man and one woman—additional little wives were no longer acceptable.

Definitely Not For Better and For Worse

Men in traditional China could divorce their first wives for six basic reasons, other than barrenness. A wife was in trouble if she was a flirt, a thief, overly talkative or prone to jealousy, if she did not listen to her in-laws or if she somehow acquired leprosy. A concubine, however, could be sent away at any time.

Keep it Simple

Although the Prophet Muhammad had 11 wives, traditionally, Muslim men are only allowed four wives at once. Each wife must be treated equally, so taking on more than one wife is an expensive undertaking. Today, most Muslim men only marry once.

Bigamy is having one spouse too many. Monogamy is the same.

—Oscar Wilde, British playwright

HOW YOUNG IS TOO YOUNG?

Because physical and emotional development varies from person to person, it's difficult to comment on what is and is not an appropriate age for young people to tie the knot. It's generally accepted in the medical world that pregnancy and childbirth are excessively demanding on young girls. With that in mind, most countries steer toward making sure that, before marrying, the young lady has at least hit her mid-teens and has parental consent or is at the age of majority, if parental consent is not available.

Just Say No to Child Marriage

Some historians suggest the practice of child marriage, not uncommon even today in parts of India, originated as a way for parents to protect their young daughters. They point back to the Muslim invasions of the Indian subcontinent more than 1000 years ago as the initiating factor in this now-illegal practice. Apparently, invaders raped and abducted young girls, and to prevent this from happening, those in some Hindu communities started marrying off their daughters as soon as they could, even at birth! Of course, this led to other problems, not the least of which was having very young girls get pregnant and dying in childbirth. To counteract the practice, the Child Marriage Restraint Act was instituted by the British government in 1929 and put in place for "the whole of India (except the State of Jammu and Kashmir), and it applies also to all citizens of India without and beyond India." Over the years, this Act has been amended numerous times. India's parliament officially adopted the Act in 1978.

Of More than just Minor Importance

The standard age for obtaining a marriage license in the U.S. is 18. (However, in Mississippi, parental consent is required for anyone under the age of 21.) Many states allow 16- and 17-year-olds to marry with parental consent. According to the National Association of Wedding Ministries, in the following states, age provisions for legal marriage are even less restrictive:

Alabama: 14, with parental consent

Georgia: younger than 16 with a court order, or without parental consent if the girl is pregnant

Hawaii: 15, with a court order

Kentucky: younger than 16 with a court order

Maryland: 15, with a court order if the girl is pregnant

Massachusetts: 12 (female) and 14 (male), with parental consent and a court order

Michigan: younger than 15 with parental consent and a court order

Minnesota: younger than 15 with parental consent and a court order

New Hampshire: 13 (female) and 14 (male), with parental consent and a waiver

New Jersey: younger than 16, if the girl is pregnant

New Mexico: 15, with a court order

New York: 14, with parental consent and approval from a Supreme Court or Family Court justice

North Carolina: 14, with notarized parental consent and a court order

Pennsylvania: younger than 16, only with parental consent and approval from a judge of the Orphans' Court

South Carolina: 14 (female), with parental consent

Tennessee: younger than 16, only with parental consent

Texas: 14, with parental consent and a court order

Utah: 14, with parental consent and approval from Juvenile Court

DID YOU KNOW?

Las Vegas might be one of the most popular quickie wedding destinations in the world, but its home state of Nevada has some of the most stringent marriage rules in the U.S. Marriage license applicants must be 21 years old or at least 16 and have parental consent. Common-law, proxy and first-cousin marriages are all prohibited.

The Canadian Way

Canadian youth are treated equally, in that, to marry, young people of both sexes must be at least 16 and have parental consent; 18-year-olds can tie the knot without parental approval. The 16- and 18-year age marks are echoed throughout most European countries, with some exceptions made for "extraordinary circumstances," such as pregnancy.

> Chester: "Marriages are very healthy, sir. You see, married men live much longer than bachelors."
>
> Tom: "If that's true, they're only trying to outlive their wives so they can be bachelors again."
>
> –Tom Bowen (Fred Astaire) and Chester the valet (Alex Frazer), *Royal Wedding* (1951)

THE PRENUP

As Sir Paul McCartney learned the hard way with his 2008 divorce from Heather Mills, a prenuptial agreement is always a good idea if you want to protect your assets in the event of a split. It's not just about capping alimony payments anymore. Modern prenups can cover everything from the religion in which the children are raised to who gets custody of the cat. They can regulate in writing how frequently visits from the in-laws will be permitted, as well as how many times per week sex is guaranteed. Some contracts go so far as to specify sexual positions! File that one under "First sign that your fiancé is a control freak!"

While not all of the following are legally enforceable, here are some of the unusual clauses that have been attached to prenuptial agreements.

Payment per Pound

In one prenuptial agreement, if the marriage fails, the wife must pay $500 for each pound (.45 kilogram) gained over her wedding weight. Another contract imposes a maximum weight of 180 pounds (82 kilograms) for the husband.

The Bad Boy Clause

Otherwise known as "fling fees," the husband is required to pay his spouse for each proven act of infidelity during the marriage. Rumor has it that Catherine Zeta-Jones insisted on this provision in her prenup to Michael Douglas—reportedly to the tune of $5 million per extramarital indiscretion! Zeta-Jones also supposedly accrues $1.5 million for each year they are married.

Pay as You Go

Apparently, Tom Cruise is "showing Katie Holmes the money." Should they divorce, she earns $3 million for every year of marriage, plus a California mansion. And if Katie Holmes can somehow manage to make it to her 11th anniversary (a feat Nicole Kidman came oh-so-close to achieving), she could hit the jackpot and get half of the actor's entire fortune.

The Cordiality Amendment

One husband is fined $10,000 every time he is rude to his wife's parents. For some mysterious reason, the wife plies her spouse with alcohol around the holidays and hovers nearby with a tape recorder.

Random Drug Testing

Every time the spouse tests positive, he pays a fine. Reportedly, Nicole Kidman's prenup includes consequences if hubby Keith Urban is caught using.

Really Tricky to Abide by During Play-offs

One poor sports fan's prenup allocates him only one football game to watch every Sunday.

Two souls with but a single thought,
Two hearts that beat as one.

– Joseph von Münch-Bellinghausen, Austrian dramatist

WHAT'S LEGAL, WHAT ISN'T?

Canadian and American legal systems address plenty of marital issues, including what constitutes a legal marriage. For example, joining two Nashville cousins in holy matrimony? Legal. Exchanging your vows over the Internet? Not legal.

A Family Affair

Ushers won't have to worry about whether to seat relatives on the bride's side or the groom's side! In Colorado and Tennessee, first cousins can legally marry. The same is true in Rhode Island, where it's also possible for a Jewish woman to legally marry her uncle; a Jewish man, however, cannot marry his aunt. In other states, marriage is permitted if cousins are more than 50 years old (Illinois), more than 65 years old (Indiana and Arizona), if one cousin is unable to reproduce (Arizona) or if both cousins are over 55 years of age and unable to reproduce (Utah).

DID YOU KNOW?

One notorious barrier-breaking groom was "Great Balls of Fire" singer and pianist Jerry Lee Lewis, whose third wife, Myra Brown, was his 13-year-old cousin (Lewis was 22 at the time). To no one's surprise, the union did not last. Lewis married a total of six wives.

Having a Gay Time in Provincetown

On May 18, 2004, Massachusetts became the first U.S. state to legally allow same-sex marriage. As long as both consenting adults are residents of Massachusetts (or another state that recognizes same-sex marriage) and they apply for the marriage license in person with proper birth and medical certificates, they qualify for this unprecedented union after a three-day waiting period. Both partners are then eligible for the same legal rights and benefits of couples in traditional marriages. That street goes both ways, however; they also can be subject to spousal support should the marriage fail.

Countries that have sanctioned same-sex marriage include the Netherlands (2001), Belgium (2003), Canada (2005) and Spain (2005). In November 2008, constitutional bans on same-sex marriage were passed in California, Arizona and Florida.

Going to the Cyber Chapel…Gonna Get Married…

…But it's not going to be legal. In the Internet era, cyber weddings are increasingly popular. However, even though vows are exchanged, these virtual marriages are not legally binding. Still, they are fun for couples wanting to include in the ceremony far-flung friends and family who aren't physically able to attend the wedding. Cyber weddings are even being used by high school couples who want to make a melodramatic commitment that's one step beyond a promise ring and a letter jacket.

Virtually Married

A basic wedding package from chatalot.com includes the use of one of the site's chapels for 24 hours with a private password for you and up to 30 guests. Depending on your personal style, you can choose from the Enchanted Chapel, the Las Vegas Chapel, the Country Chapel, the International Chapel and the Gothic Chapel. You also are entitled to a reserved honeymoon suite with a private password for one week. Use your imagination as to what exactly that entails.

Hope for Lonely Web Surfers

The perfect candidates for cyber weddings? According to Internet matchmaking service eHarmony, 236 users of its website marry each year! (Real weddings, not the cyber variety.)

You were born together, and together you shall be for evermore...but let there be spaces in your togetherness. And let the winds of the heavens dance between you.

–Kahlil Gibran, Lebanese-American author

MONEY, MONEY, MONEY

Weddings are a $161-billion industry. It is estimated that more than two million weddings will take place in the United States in 2009, each costing an average of $30,860, an increase of 11 percent from 2007. Other areas of excessive inflation? Most marriage licenses cost at least 500 percent more today than they did 50 years ago, when they were around one dollar. And postage for those invitations has skyrocketed—in 1958, it was only four cents per envelope! E-vites, anyone?

Break It Down

What eats up the biggest chunk of your wedding budget? The reception, of course. Following are the approximate average costs, in U.S. dollars, for the wedding components, in order, from most to least expensive.

Reception (including food, drink, cake, venue)	$14,000
Honeymoon	$3,600
Photography/videography	$3,600
Wedding attire (bride and groom)	$2,600
Wedding rings	$2,100
Flowers	$2,000
Wedding gifts (for wedding party, party favors)	$1,100
Invitations	$850

DID YOU  KNOW?

In U.S. dollars, the average cost of a Japanese wedding is $93,750.

Who Pays for What?

These days, anything goes. Because couples are marrying older, when they're more likely to be financially secure, the bride and groom often pitch in for some or even all of the wedding costs. In other cases, because of the skyrocketing expenses attached to a wedding, the groom's family often takes on some of the financial responsibility. Following are the expenses traditionally covered by the bride and her family, according to etiquette expert Emily Post:

☛ services of a traditional wedding consultant, if hired

☛ invitations, enclosures and announcements

☛ the bride's wedding gown and accessories

☛ floral decorations for the ceremony and reception, the bridesmaids' flowers and the bride's bouquet

☛ formal wedding photographs and candid pictures

☛ video of the wedding, if optioned

☛ music for the church and reception

☛ transportation of the bridal party to and from the ceremony

☛ all reception expenses

☛ the bride's gifts to her attendants

☛ the bride's gift to the groom

☛ the groom's wedding ring

☛ rental of an awning for the ceremony entrance, if needed, and carpet for the aisle

☛ services of a traffic officer or parking attendants

☛ transportation of the bridal party

- transportation and lodging expenses for the officiant if from another town and if invited to officiate by the bride's family

- accommodations for the bridal attendants

- the bridesmaids' luncheon

Traditional Expenses of the Groom and His Family

- the bride's engagement and wedding rings

- the groom's gift to the bride

- gifts for the groom's attendants

- ties and gloves for the groom's attendants, if they're not part of the clothing rental package

- the bride's bouquet (only where it is local custom for the groom to pay for it)

- the bride's going-away corsage

- boutonnieres for the groom's attendants

- corsages for immediate members of both families (unless the bride has included them in her florist's order)

- the officiant's fee or donation

- transportation and lodging expenses for the officiant, if from another town and if invited to officiate by the groom's family

- the marriage license

- transportation for the groom and best man to the ceremony

- honeymoon expenses

- all costs of the rehearsal dinner

- accommodations for the groom's attendants

- the bachelor dinner, if the groom wishes to give one

- transportation and lodging expenses for the groom's family

Bridesmaids' and Honor Attendants' Expenses

- the purchase of apparel and all accessories

- transportation to and from the city in which the wedding takes place

- a contribution to a gift from all the bridesmaids to the bride

- an individual gift to the couple

- optionally, a shower or luncheon for the bride

Best Man's, Groomsmen's and Ushers' Expenses

- the rental or purchase of wedding attire

- transportation to and from the city in which the wedding takes place

- a contribution to a gift from all the groom's attendants to the groom

- an individual gift to the couple

- a bachelor dinner, if given by the groom's attendants

Out-of-Town Guests' Expenses

- transportation to and from the wedding

- lodging expenses and meals

- wedding gift

Most Expensive Wedding in the World

Indian steel magnate Lakshmi Mittal holds the record for financing the most expensive wedding ever—to the tune of US$60 million. His precious daughter Vanisha, then 23 years old, wed Amit Bhatia, 25, on June 22, 2004 in front of more than 1000 guests. It was an elaborate (to say the least) six-day celebration, with chateau hopping from Versailles to Paris. Not surprisingly, proud papa Mittal has frequently made *Forbes* magazine's list of richest people in the world, coming in at number five in 2007. He also held a world record for most-expensive house.

> George: *"What is that twelve hundred? Is that DOLLARS? Twelve hundred DOLLARS! My first car didn't cost that much."*
>
> Franck: *"Well…welcome to the nineties, Mr. Banks!"*
>
> —George Banks (Steve Martin) and wedding planner Franck Eggelhoffer (Martin Short) picking out a cake, *Father of the Bride* (1991)

HOW TO MARRY, IF NOT A MILLIONAIRE

The average household income of today's American newlyweds is $60,000. Add up the cost of an average wedding, which includes expenses for photographers, flowers, food, the reception hall, the dress, plus more, and the nuptials eat up a substantial piece of the income pie. Most couples are faced with the realization that they simply cannot have it all and are forced to make concessions. Of course, the art of compromise is a necessity for a lasting marriage, so perhaps it's just as well that the bride and groom get some practice when planning the wedding. Or, they could, like plenty of couples, devise ways to have the wedding of their dreams without breaking the bank.

This Wedding has Been Brought to You By...

If you are not one of the richest people in the world nor even in the top 50th percentile of your town, one way to cover the wedding expenses is to have your wedding sponsored. The concept was the brainchild of Philadelphia entrepreneur Tom Anderson. In 1999, he was trying to juggle launching a business and planning a wedding, and he realized the two endeavors had one glaring commonality—they needed capital. He pounded the pavement and persuaded about two dozen companies to contribute to his $30,000 big day. Since then, sponsored weddings have become increasingly popular. As Star Jones went on and on (and on and on) on *The View* about her wedding plans to Al Reynolds, she made no secret of the fact that they were paying for practically nothing.

Fundraising

When savvy Ohio resident Christina Fanizzi was planning her nuptials, she used her sales skills to negotiate corporate sponsorships covering 80 percent of her wedding's $15,000 price tag. Which is not to say it came easy. She estimated that she invested six to eight hours a day, Monday through Friday, pitching to potential sponsors. However, some publicity-hungry businesses are perfectly happy to get involved. In exchange for goods, services or cash, the corporate logo is often included on invitations, programs, thank-you cards and even matchbooks and party favors.

It's True: You Really Can Buy Anything on eBay

A more recent example of the sponsored wedding trend happened in June 2008. For their April 2009 wedding, Virginia Beach hairdresser Kelly Gray and her fiancé, Karl Gau, set a budget of $7000 (about the cost of the confetti tossed around at Lakshmi Mittal's daughter's wedding). With a combined annual income of $32,000 and a one-year-old daughter to support, the young couple knew they would have to cut corners and be creative. One of Gray's bridesmaids suggested they auction off a bridesmaid spot on eBay. The listing started at a penny and was soon up to more than $200. The winning bidder would receive a bridesmaid dress and shoes and an invitation for two to attend the wedding, along with a role in the ceremony. Many women groan at the obligation (and unflattering gown) associated with being a bridesmaid, so who could have predicted it would be such a hot commodity on the World Wide Web? The final bid: $5700! The winner was drpeppersnapple, otherwise known as the Dr. Pepper Snapple Group. The soft drink conglomerate even generously offered to up their sponsorship to a cool $10,000. As of press time, the company had not announced who would stand up at the wedding. A Diet Raspberry Iced Tea Snapple says it turns out to be Wendy Kaufman, the annoying Snapple Lady from the old commercials.

Cost Crunching

Money-conscious brides and grooms are seeking increasingly creative solutions to budget challenges. Here are some cost-crunching strategies.

☛ Have one small, lovely cake made for show but serve the masses from a hidden plain sheet cake. Or partially construct the showy cake from polystyrene—rarely will a guest notice the difference!

☛ Forgo the traditional band or DJ; instead, load up an iPod with your favorite songs and hook it up to some speakers.

☛ In-season flowers are less expensive than exotic, out-of-season blooms. Fill out the bouquets with more greens, ribbons or baby's breath.

☛ Eliminate those disposable cameras on the table. They scarcely produce any photos worth the cost of developing. No cameras means no time wasted sorting through a lot of poorly shot or unused film.

☛ Skimp on party favors. More than half the guests will leave them at the reception hall, anyway. Who needs a hundred leftover mint boxes (or matchbooks or coasters or picture frames) with names on them?

☛ Handwritten or mass-produced computerized invitations can be acceptable, if created with loving care.

DID YOU  **KNOW?**

According to the financial experts at the Motley Fool, instead of spending $25,000 on your wedding, you can marry at city hall and invest the $25,000 in S&P 500 index funds. After 40 years, you and your spouse will have more than a million dollars!

Protecting your Investment

With some weddings costing more than a car, some couples are making the sensible decision to invest in insurance. A wedding insurance policy starts at about $195 and, depending on the options selected by the purchaser, can cover cancellation or postponement scenarios such as natural disasters, additional expenses (such as the caterer not showing up, so you have to pay double to book another one at the last minute); new attire, should anything happen to the dress or tuxedos; photography, if something happens to the photos; and rental property, should it be damaged during the reception. Almost the only contingency not covered is a change of heart. Many wedding insurance policies feature a "cold-feet exclusion."

Marrying a man is like buying something you've been admiring for a long time in a shop window. You may love it when you get home, but it doesn't always go with everything else in the house.

–Jean Kerr, American author and playwright

THE WEDDING PARTY

*The custom of the bride and groom having attendants—friends
who stand up to support them during their exchange of wedding
vows—is about as old as the practice of marriage itself.*

Evading Evil

Bridesmaids during the early Roman era were usually chosen
from the bride's relatives or closest friends. Their roles, however,
were an interesting blend of the practical and the superstitious.
Moral support and help in planning the upcoming wedding
were among the practical concerns, but bridesmaids were also
used as decoys, to confuse evil spirits that might want to attack
the bride or harm the couple. During the wedding ceremony,
the attendants were dressed in a fashion similar or identical to
the bride and groom for this very purpose. It became Roman
law for a wedding to have 10 witnesses to ward off malevolent
spirits attempting to bring bad luck to the newlyweds.
Interestingly enough, the belief that evil spirits or, at the very
least, folks who didn't wish the couple the best of luck, could
curse the wedding continued well into the Victorian era.

Don't Look Back

Another traditional responsibility of the best man was to protect
the groom and his betrothed by warding off potential bad luck.
The groomsman did this by carrying a charm in his pocket and
making darned sure that, once the groom started out for the
church, he didn't turn back—not even if he'd forgotten something as important as the rings!

DID YOU KNOW?

Some cultures do not believe in offering such extensive help to
the couple. Traditional German brides have no attendants,
except a flower girl.

Extra Support

In a traditional Hispanic wedding, a well-established couple in the family's circle is chosen to be sponsors or godparents for the bride and groom. The role is a huge honor, as well as a large responsibility. They are expected to provide emotional and spiritual support, from the time of the engagement to several years after the couple is married. Those of us who are familiar with those first few rough years of marriage know what a blessing this tradition must be! These godparents can also be called on to provide some financial support, and, during the wedding, they have clearly defined roles: the godfather (*padrino*) has the honor of walking the bride down the aisle; the godmother (*madrina*) supplies the couple's kneeling cushion for Mass.

DID YOU  KNOW?

The average wedding party consists of 12 members. A flower girl is featured in 62 percent of weddings, and 56 percent have a ring bearer.

Marriage—a book of which the first chapter is written in poetry and the remaining chapters written in prose.

–Beverley Nichols, British author

WITH THIS RING

That the exchanging of wedding rings is an important part of many formal weddings is common knowledge, but have you ever wondered how the tradition began and about its signifi-cance to the wearer? Scholars believe the custom of exchanging wedding rings began in ancient Egypt and that it really has nothing to do with Judeo-Christian traditions, as some might think. The first time rings were exchanged during a wedding ceremony—at least, the first time such an occasion was recorded—was in Egypt, about 4800 years ago. Initially, the unbroken circle of the ring was thought to represent everlasting love, and in the Egyptian tradition, the ring was tied to the supernatural. Later, a Roman bride wore a ring to signify that she was no longer in the single's market. Because of these ancient roots, the early Christian church initially rejected the idea of a wedding ring, considering it a pagan tradition.

Big Diamond Theory?

In addition to its timeless durability, a diamond can be considered a symbol of life. New research suggests that diamonds might, in fact, have played a part in the origin of life on Earth. Diamonds are crystallized forms of carbon that predate the oldest known forms of life on the planet. A trio of German scientists, Andrei Sommer, Dan Zhu, and Hans-Joerg Fecht, posed a theory suggesting that, billions of years ago, primitive molecules landed on hydrogenated diamonds, and the reaction generated complex organic molecules capable of creating life!

DID YOU  **KNOW?**

In prehistoric times, women were often reluctantly yoked to their mates by a rope or chain, making the "ring" a rather cumbersome symbol of love and fidelity.

Common Bond

In Egypt, it was once traditional for a man to place ring money, an ancient coin resembling a ring, on his bride's finger to signify that his property and income were now held in common with his new wife.

DID YOU  **KNOW?**

It was not until World War II, when men left their wives to serve overseas, that it was fashionable for men to wear wedding rings. The ring was a sign of hope and a reminder of happier times.

Designating the Ring Finger

The practice of wearing a wedding ring on the third finger of
the left hand has been common in the Roman world since its
earliest days. The third finger, also known as the vein finger by
several cultures, was chosen because it was believed that the
blood flowing through that vein ran directly to the heart.

Key Ring

In the Roman Empire, a groom did not present his bride with
a ring until she was brought to the couple's new home. The
wedding ring was often made from the key to the room in
which he kept his worldly goods. The giving of the ring signified a sharing of his home and wealth with his new bride and
that she owned the key to his heart.

DID YOU  KNOW?

At one time, Roman wedding rings were carved to represent
two clasped hands.

And the Band Played On

When England was still ironing out the kinks of becoming a
country in its own right, the practice of giving a wedding ring
was just coming into vogue. It was a long time, however, before
the practice was universally accepted. In fact, the Puritans, who
firmly believed that all jewelry belonged to Satan, absolutely
prohibited the giving of a wedding ring. As the custom slowly
became accepted, the next hurdle to overcome was deciding
which finger should bear the ring. For a while, it was customary
to put the ring on the ring finger of the bride's right hand, but
that changed sometime during the Reformation.

Making it Official

In the Jewish tradition, a plain gold ring is given by the *chatan* (groom) to his *kallah* (bride) and placed on the forefinger of her right hand. This action symbolizes that the couple is officially wed. The kallah might also present the chatan with a ring, but this is not part of the official ceremony and does not take place until a later date, often privately.

Close to the Heart

Gold is the traditional symbol of marriage in India, but it takes more forms than the usual wedding ring. A gold pendant hung on a simple thread is called the *mangalsutra* or *thaali*—it's known by different terms in different areas of India. In a Hindu wedding ceremony, the groom hangs the thaali around the bride's neck. Another traditional Indian love token, again presented by the groom to his new bride, is the toe ring. The groom places a ring on one or more of his bride's toes.

The Strong Arm

In Greece, the wedding ring is traditionally worn on the ring finger of the right hand. This is because Greeks consider the right hand to be the strong, dominant hand. German couples also traditionally wore their wedding rings on their right hands. The rings were identical, plain bands without diamonds.

DID YOU  **KNOW?**

One superstition states that it is good luck to receive an engagement ring sporting the recipient's birthstone.

Hand in Hand

In Polish weddings, another symbolic uniting of husband and wife was tradition long before rings were introduced into that culture. A hand-binding ceremony saw the young couple join their hands over a loaf of bread. A specially made, embroidered cloth was used to bind their hands together, symbolizing that they were united in all aspects of life. This quaint tradition was originally part of a formal engagement ceremony. However, it was considered as binding as the marriage itself and, over the years, has been adopted as part of a traditional Polish wedding ceremony.

Double Meaning

The Irish Claddagh ring, sporting the design of a crowned heart held by a pair of hands, was designed in the 16th century. Although not traditionally a wedding ring, it was worn with the heart pointing away from the body by single folks looking for love. Once taken, the wearer turned the ring around, so the heart pointed toward the heart. The Claddagh is sometimes still the wedding ring of choice for those wanting a traditional Celtic wedding experience.

Saying it with Jade

Although the exchange of wedding rings isn't a Chinese tradition, that culture does attach a different meanings to each finger. The third finger of the left hand is said to represent one's "life partner." It makes sense, then, that Chinese partners who choose to exchange rings wear them on that finger.

Other traditions common to a number of Asian cultures are the exchange of jade and the giving of a pearl ring. Jade represents health, luck and prosperity, and the exchange of jade between marrying families signifies a warm welcome. Although, in some traditions, pearls are considered a sign of tears, the Asian practice of the groom giving pearls to the bride is a tradition that has gained momentum in the Western world, as well.

Papal Approval

The church did not officially sanction engagement rings until 860 AD, when Pope Nicholas I declared that a ring given to a maiden signified the intent of marriage. The ring represented a financial sacrifice for the gent proposing.

Three in One

The wedding ring holds a deep religious significance in a traditional Russian ceremony. In that culture, a wedding band is composed of three interlocked rings in three colors of gold, representing God the Father, God the Son and God the Holy Spirit.

A Triune Prayer

The Holy Trinity was also invoked during a wedding ceremony through the use of a wedding band in medieval England. During that time, it was customary for a bridegroom to place his bride's wedding band first on her thumb, then on each of the following two fingers, while saying "In the name of the Father, the Son and the Holy Ghost" with each finger, after which the ring came to its final home on the third finger. This tradition was written into the Book of Common Prayer, the prayer book of the Church of England, in the 1500s.

Some Now, Some Later

In Muslim tradition, a contract between the bride and groom specifies the monetary amount the groom promises his bride. This is usually provided in a two-installment gift plan. The ring often serves as the "prompt," or down-payment, if you will, given before consummation of the marriage. After the wedding, a follow-up gift is given.

Floral Formality

In Hindu ceremonies, it is customary for the bride and groom to exchange garlands of flowers in lieu of, or in addition to, rings; the garlands are worn for the duration of the ceremony. This is similar to a custom commonly practiced in modern Hawaiian weddings. Insert your own lei joke here.

DID YOU  KNOW?

Swedish wives sometimes wear three wedding rings, for betrothal, for marriage and for motherhood.

Inscriptions

Engraving the inside of a wedding ring with a special saying is yet another wedding convention that came into vogue during the reign of Queen Victoria. Even before Queen Victoria popularized it, some betrothed couples in 18th-century Ireland took the letters from their names, mixed them up or intertwined them, then had the letters engraved into the rings. Many couples choose initials, dates or poetic phrases. King Edward VIII had the phrase "We are ours now, 27 x 36" carved into the ring for his beloved Wallis Simpson. The numbers refer to October 27, 1936, the date Simpson's divorce proceedings from her husband began. Princess Diana's gold wedding ring from Prince Charles simply read, "I love you, Diana." Tony Parker and Eva Longoria have a private inscription in French, Parker's native language, engraved into each of their Piaget white-gold wedding bands. Courteney Cox and David Arquette reportedly have the phrase "A Deal's a Deal" engraved into their wedding bands.

Ring, Nerd-Style

One of the most original, and by far geekiest, wedding ring inscriptions was created by Jakob Homan. The University of Washington computer and software systems student proudly wears a titanium wedding band that he had inscribed with a message in binary code: "01001010 01010011." He claims the code is easy to decipher. Um, maybe if you're a computer and software systems student. Perhaps his wife's wedding band is a decoder ring.

And the Man shall give unto the Woman a Ring, laying the same upon the book with the accustomed duty to the Priest and Clerk. And the Priest, taking the Ring, shall deliver it unto the Man, to put it upon the fourth finger of the Woman's left hand. And the Man holding the Ring there, and taught by the Priest, shall say, "With this ring I thee wed…"

—Book of Common Prayer, 1962

MUSIC FOR GETTING MARRIED

We've all heard them—know them from the first few bars of music—but where did the "Bridal Chorus" and "Wedding March" come from, and how did they become a part of wedding traditions the world over? And how about some less-traditional wedding music?

Bridal Chorus

The "Bridal Chorus" comes from German composer Richard Wagner's opera, *Lohengrin*. Written in 1850, the renowned piece plays during Act III, Scene I, when Elsa and her new husband enter the bridal chamber. The music, along with the romantic opera, so captivated the imaginations of audiences that it has since been used to announce the bride's trip down the aisle to her betrothed.

Wedding March

Felix Mendelssohn is credited with composing the "Wedding March," the piece traditionally played after the bridal vows are exchanged and while the couple makes the joint trip back down the aisle and out of the church. Typically referred to as the recessional, Mendelssohn's masterpiece was originally composed for the stage production of William Shakespeare's *A Midsummer Night's Dream* in 1842.

Here Comes the Bride

The "Bridal Chorus" and the "Wedding March" were first paired at the wedding of Queen Victoria's daughter, Vicky, when she wed German prince Friedrich Wilhelm of Prussia on January 25, 1858. It rapidly became fashionable to use these compositions at other weddings. Prior to this, music was not considered appropriate during a church service.

Canon in D Major

In an effort to switch it up a bit, after 150-plus years of the Wagner and Mendelssohn music tradition, couples started using Johann Pachelbel's *Canon in D Major* as a processional option. It is interesting to note, however, that Pachelbel's creation was written sometime around 1680—almost two centuries before Queen Victoria's darling daughter first made wedding music popular. The *Canon*, an extraction from the Baroque period, was originally composed for three violins and basso continuo.

DID YOU KNOW?

If you want Elton John to perform at your wedding, be prepared to shell out at least two million British pounds, as Peter Shalson did for his and his new wife's 300 guests. For further eclectic entertainment, Shalson procured Kool and the Gang and members of *The Lion King*'s London West End cast.

Beware of Journey?

A song by Journey ("Don't Stop Believing") is known for scoring the controversially abrupt ending of *The Sopranos* television series. Coincidentally, songs by the group have been prominent in weddings whose marriages have ended just as suddenly. Britney Spears and Kevin Federline danced to "Lights" (a.k.a. "City by the Bay"), and Charlie Sheen and Denise Richards selected "Open Arms."

A Better Choice Than "You Give Love a Bad Name"

They'd better hold on to what they've got. Andrew Firestone, former contestant on *The Bachelor*, might not have found love on television, but, on July 5, 2008, he married model Ivana Bozilovic at St. Mark's in the Valley Episcopal Church in Los Olivos, California. The ceremony came to an end to the strains of their recessional song—none other than Bon Jovi's '80s classic "Livin' on a Prayer." Lyric sheets were passed around, and 300 guests sang and shouted the words aloud. Hey, they've got each other, and that's a lot.

Another Bachelor's Musical Choice: The Boss

Firestone's *Bachelor* predecessor Bob Guiney married *All My Children* actress Rebecca Budig at a very low-key Fourth of July weekend ceremony in Long Lake, Michigan. The wedding included a homestyle barbecue and swim apparel. And the bride's song as she walked down the aisle? "Thunder Road," the Bruce Springsteen ballad from his 1975 *Born to Run* album. Lyrics such as "you ain't a beauty, but hey, you're all right" might make this a less-than-traditional wedding tune. But it also promises "Show a little faith; there's magic in the night."

Foreign Film

The theme song from the film *Cinema Paradiso* was selected for the weddings of both actress Rena Sofer and her producer/director hubby Sanford Bookstaver and by *Passions* actress (and daughter of soap opera queen Susan Lucci) Liza Huber and her spouse, Alex Hesterberg III. Comedian Adam Sandler and wife Jackie Titone also went with the theme from an Italian Academy Award–winning foreign film: their wedding featured the theme from *Life is Beautiful*.

The Glory of Love

The "Asian chic" wedding between journalist Lisa Ling and oncologist Paul Song was atypical in just about every aspect. The ushers wore Cobra Kai uniforms straight out of *The Karate Kid*, and the bride wore red. And, although the vows were punctuated by Tupac Shakur's "California Love" set to a banging gong, the bride and groom also entertained guests with a performance of Sonny and Cher's "I Got You Babe."

More Unconventional Musical Choices

☛ Although "I'll Be There for You" would have also been apropos, *Friends* actress Courteney Cox and her *Scream* costar David Arquette selected Paul McCartney and Wings' "Maybe I'm Amazed" for their wedding.

☛ For their recessional "hymn," Emmy-winning *Law and Order: Special Victims Unit* actress (and Jayne Mansfield's daughter) Mariska Hargitay and beau Peter Hermann chose "Ain't No Mountain High Enough" by Diana Ross and the Supremes.

☛ Exhibiting similar exuberance, actors William H. Macy and Felicity Huffman picked "I Feel Good" by James Brown.

☛ The July 2007 wedding of Jerry O'Connell and Rebecca Romijn was a Western-style backyard affair, complete with hay bales and wagon wheels. After saying "I do," the couple proceeded down the aisle (grass) accompanied by a gospel choir's rendition of the 5th Dimension's "Let the Sunshine In."

☛ From *Saved by the Bell* to dancing around a pole: *Showgirls* actress Elizabeth Berkley wed painter Greg Lauren in 2003, and their first dance (which, presumably did not involve a pole or pasties) was to Madonna's "Crazy for You."

☛ "Overjoyed" by Stevie Wonder was the wedding song for the 2003 nuptials of early *Rent* co-stars Taye Diggs and Idina Menzel. (Fun wedding fact: Diggs and Menzel married at the Round Hill Hotel and Villas in Montego Bay, Jamaica, the Caribbean locale where Diggs' character, Winston Shakespeare, romanced Angela Bassett's Stella in the film version of *How Stella Got her Groove Back*.)

DID YOU  KNOW?

One of the most popular wedding songs for celebrities and real people alike is the Etta James classic "At Last." It was featured in the weddings of Ashton Kutcher and Demi Moore, Christina Aguilera and Jordan Bratman, news anchor Elizabeth Vargas and Marc Cohn, and Scott Wolf (*Party of Five*) and *Real World* alum Kelley Limp.

> *"When I lived in Porpoise Spit, I used to sit in my room for hours and listen to ABBA songs. But since I've met you and moved to Sydney, I haven't listened to one ABBA song. That's because my life is as good as an ABBA song. It's as good as 'Dancing Queen.'"*

–Muriel Heslop (Toni Collette), *Muriel's Wedding* (1994)

THE FLOWERS

Although brides did not always carry a bouquet of flowers on their wedding day, the presence of flowers in the planning and preparations for an upcoming wedding has a longstanding tradition.

Evil Be Gone

Among the many precautions brides and grooms took to ensure
that evil spirits did not attack them on their way to the altar,
from as far back as Roman times, was the use of herbs, spices
and other flora. It was believed that their strong scent warded
off these evil spirits, along with any bad luck that might lurk
about. Usually, these herbs and flowers were woven into wreaths
or garlands worn by the bride and groom. The circular shape of
the wreath also symbolized "new life, hope and fertility."

The Meaning of Flowers

During the Victorian era, lovers exchanged flowers as a sign of
their love and commitment to each other. However, different
flowers carried different meanings. Although a red rose might
symbolize love and passion, a pink rose signified that dreaded
"friend" title. If you didn't trust your suitor, the flower to
deliver was indisputably lavender, because it traditionally indicated distrust. And a yellow chrysanthemum found on your
doorstep could have you thinking for days, because that particular bloom meant you had a secret admirer.

MultiHortiCultural Weddings

Brides took great pains to ensure that the flowers they included
in their bouquets held special meaning for the couple. Flowers
and plants such as ivy (symbolizing fidelity), hydrangea (perse-
verance), holly (domestic happiness) and hyacinth (domestic
happiness) were particularly popular. According to Scottish lore,
it was lucky for a bride to carry a sprig of heather in her bouquet. Often, the bride would retain the dried heather for years
as a wedding memento.

The Power of Orange

For traditional Spanish weddings, brides chose orange blossoms, in reference to orange trees, which are capable of simultaneously bearing both fruit and blossoms. It was believed that a bride carrying orange blossoms would experience both happiness and fulfillment.

Polish Wedding Floral Etiquette

Poles have long used red and white roses or tulips for bridal bouquets, paying tribute to the colors of the Polish flag. Etiquette demands that guests invited to a Polish wedding bring the bride and groom flowers. If you thought manning the guest book was an undesirable assignment, imagine the poor wedding attendants delegated to flower duty, which usually entails continuously hauling hundreds of flowers into vehicles for the after-party.

DID YOU KNOW?

Although quite trendy and stylish today, a red-and-white color scheme for flowers was once considered bad luck in many cultures. The colors represented blood and bandages.

Love at first sight is easy to understand; it's when two people have been looking at each other for a lifetime that it becomes a miracle.

—Amy Bloom, American writer

THE CEREMONY

From those first few bars of music to the final kiss, the formal ceremony joining two people together in holy matrimony has been sacred throughout history. How that takes place, whether it's a culturally driven ceremony or a modern take on an ancient theme, is as varied as the betrothed.

A Noble Act

A priest places a crown of flowers, called a *stefana*, on the heads of the bride and groom in a traditional Greek wedding ceremony. This act of "crowning" emphasizes the solemnity of marriage, and the two crowns are joined by white ribbon, representing the union of man and wife. The *koumbaro* and *koumbara* (best man and maid of honor) rotate the crowns from bride to groom three times, to represent the Holy Trinity: God the Father, God the Son and God the Holy Ghost. The Trinity is symbolically evoked at least twice more during the ceremony, once when the priest leads the bride, groom and attendants around the altar three times, and again when the rings are exchanged three times.

DID YOU  **KNOW?**

The tradition of the bride standing to the groom's left during the wedding ceremony originated centuries ago. It was so the groom could protect his bride by quickly reaching for his sword with his right hand, if necessary.

Handfasting

It was not always customary for a priest or other religious representative to officiate over a wedding ceremony in Great Britain. It was simply not practical in some areas, especially in rural areas, in which a visit from a priest was a rarity. Instead, a couple wishing to marry joined their right and left hands together in the presence of family, friends and official witnesses and pledged their love to each another. The joining of the hands formed a figure eight, resembling an infinity symbol, to suggest that the couple's love would last forever. This handfasting ceremony was only a temporary wedding ceremony, however, and the couple had to renew their vows within a year and a day—or 13 moon cycles—of their first exchange. If the marriage lasted that long, the couple could renew their vows for a lifetime or, according to some historians, for "as long as love shall last."

Later, when it became fashionable for a priest to preside over a wedding, handfasting was used as a temporary marriage until the priest made his annual visit to the area. The handfasting ceremony is commonly considered the original vow-renewal ceremony.

In a variation of handfasting, family and friends attending the ceremony bind the couple's hands together with strips of material or ribbons. Hence, the origins of the popular phrase "tying the knot."

Jumping the Sword

In Canadian military weddings, the newlywed couple holds hands in front of a sword laid on the floor. A corporal or sergeant acting as the clergyman orders (using rather unique "terms of endearment") the couple to "Leap, rogue, and jump, whore, and then you are married forevermore," while a drum beats. They are considered husband and wife once they leap together over the sword.

Jumping in with Both Feet

In the early history of the United States, when keeping African slaves was still a common practice, marriage was just one of the many liberties these transplanted Americans were denied. However, it was important for those who wanted to make some kind of formal commitment to their chosen partner to adopt a symbolic gesture that, at least in their minds, gave credibility to their union. And so it was that the tradition of "Jumping the Broom" was formed. A broom, which symbolized the keeping of a home, was laid on the floor. With drums beating in the background, the man and woman wanting to marry joined hands and, together, jumped over the broom and into married life. If they were available, cowrie shells were worn around the bride's neck or attached as decorations to the couple's clothing. These shells were believed to encourage fertility.

Blood Bread

In the Romani tradition, when a man and woman agree to share their life together, they are considered married. If there is any kind of a special ceremony or gathering, it is usually not faith-focused and it often takes place in front of one of the couple's elders. Over time, however, a number of more formal rites of marriage developed, two of which center on bread. In one tradition, the bride and groom each hold a piece of bread. Each partner pricks a finger and allows a drop of blood to fall onto the bread. The pieces are then exchanged, and the husband and wife consume the other's bread offering. Another interesting bread tradition requires the bride and groom to sit next to each other, surrounded by their family and friends. An appointed individual places bread and salt on the bride's knees. The groom and the bride sprinkle some of the salt on the bread and eat it. This tradition is believed to ensure the couple a happy life together.

Superstitions Run Rampant

Austrians, apparently a superstitious bunch, had a long list of do's and don'ts for a smooth wedding and a happy, successful marriage.

☛ A man preparing to propose sent a friend or family member to visit the prospective bride and her family. It was believed that if, during the journey, the designated representative encountered a monk, pregnant woman or blind man, the marriage would be cursed. On the bright side, a sighting of a goat, wolf or pigeon en route was considered good luck.

☛ Forget about those schoolgirl notebook doodlings of "Mrs. _____." A bride prematurely writing her married name was inviting bad luck. It was also deemed ill-fated for an Austrian woman to marry a man whose last name began with the same letter as hers. (Fortunately, this superstition did not apply in Asia, with its limited number of surnames, or very few marriages would take place there.)

☛ Many cultures believe it is bad luck for the groom to see the bride before the wedding, but Austrians take this superstition a step further, suggesting that the bride should not try on her entire ensemble until the day of the wedding. Some Austrian brides even left one final stitch on the dress undone until the moment before the ceremony was to begin. It is also bad fortune for the bride to make her own dress.

☛ A bride may look in the mirror before leaving for her wedding, but, once she has embarked for the ceremony, any other mirror glances could bring doom to the marriage. It was viewed as a positive omen to encounter a black cat, spider, rainbow or chimney sweep during the journey. In fact, some brides even hired a chimney sweep to cross their path, just to be safe.

☛ All marriages weather good times and bad, but Austrians believed the weather on the wedding day itself could determine the happiness of the marriage. Snow indicated fertility, wealth and health; cloudy skies and rain forecasted a stormy marriage.

☛ It was also believed that the first partner to make a purchase after the nuptials was established as the dominant one in the relationship. Many eager Austrian brides quickly purchased something small from a ready bridesmaid immediately following the ceremony.

A Stitch in Time

While visiting a traditional Belgian family, you might notice a framed bit of lace proudly displayed on the dining room wall or in some other equally prominent place in the home. On closer scrutiny, you'll see a name or two embroidered on the cloth, and, if you are really observant, you might recognize the fact that some of the crocheted cotton looks a little brighter and newer than other bits. That is because what you have uncovered is the "something old" carried by brides during a traditional Belgian wedding—a lace handkerchief with their names embroidered on it—and the brightest, newest looking name is the latest woman in the family to marry. With each family wedding, the handkerchief is removed from its glass frame, embroidered with the newest bride's name and given to her to carry throughout her wedding day. It is then returned to its glass frame and hung in the new bride's home, waiting for the next lucky lady to say, "I do."

Although it is not clear when this quaint tradition originated, it is safe to say that it has been going on for as long as anyone can remember. Some variations on the theme include embroidering the names of the entire wedding party and displaying the heirloom hankie, embroidered with all the married daughters' names, in the maternal family home, instead of in the new bride's home.

Hanky Variations

☛ The Irish, bless them, have their priorities straight when it comes to the purpose behind weddings, and it's all about babies. An Irish bride carries a special wedding hanky during her special day. What's special about it? After the wedding is over, all she needs to do is add a few stitches, and voila—the hanky is now a Christening bonnet! When that baby grows up and is old enough to marry, the bonnet can be converted back into that special wedding hanky.

☛ In China, it is traditional for brides and grooms to wish each other luck for the future by exchanging handkerchiefs after the wedding ceremony and before the evening festivities. Not just any hankies will do, however. They must be red and adorned with images of mandarin ducks, symbolizing that the couple's lifelong commitment is the same as that of the mandarin duck, which mates for life.

Extra, Extra, Read All About It!

In preparation for the wedding, friends and family of the bride and groom in Germany create a "wedding newspaper," similar to a modern scrapbook, featuring photos and stories about the couple. At the reception, the newspaper is sold to guests to raise funds for the honeymoon. The wedding festivities themselves usually last for three days. On the first day or night is a civil ceremony attended by only the couple's closest family members and friends. On the second night is the big party. It was considered good luck for guests to bring old dishes to the party and break them! The act of the newlyweds sweeping up the broken pieces was said to represent an intact household. The religious ceremony is performed on the third day of the wedding festivities. During the vows, as the couple kneels, the groom might intentionally kneel on the bride's gown to establish himself as the dominant partner in the marriage. The bride might respond by stepping on his foot as they rise, to signal that he should think again!

An often-rowdy reception follows the religious ceremony. It is traditional for the best man at some point to steal the bride away for a drink at a nearby pub until she is found by the groom! As the couple prepares to embark on the honeymoon, it is not uncommon for the groom to have to pay a "toll" for them to leave. The toll is usually a promise to hold another party on the newlyweds' return.

DID YOU  KNOW?

For many of the Samburu people of Kenya, the marriage is only finalized when a bull is sacrificed.

Shedding Light on the Matter

The tradition of lighting a candle has held significance throughout the ages. Light illuminates the darkness, chases away evil spirits hiding in the shadows and inspires a sense of hope. The lighting of candles has been a part of numerous religious ceremonies and traditions. It's no surprise, then, that the practice is part of a traditional Christian wedding ceremony. In this practice, the candle is called the "unity candle." As the mothers of the bride and groom are ushered into the church, each woman lights a candle representing her family and sets it into a candleholder. After the vows and rings are exchanged, the bride and groom take these candles and together use them to light the unity candle. They then blow out the candles lit by their mothers. This action signifies the union of the newly married couple and their intention to share their lives together. In one variation on this custom, the bride and groom each light a candle before together lighting the unity candle.

Light My Fire

Candles play an integral role in the Wiccan matrimonial ceremony. Unlike the unity candle practice, however, the Wiccan
candle-lighting ceremony includes blessings that emphasize the
independence of the bride and groom and decrees that individu-
ality is not lost in the bonds of marriage. There was reportedly
a Wiccan influence when Jim Morrison, lead singer of the
Doors, exchanged vows with journalist Patricia Kennealy in
June 1970. The Celtic Pagan ceremony incorporated both handfasting and candles.

The Fire Ceremony

One Native American ceremony uses fire to symbolize the union
of the newly married bride and groom to each other and to the
Great Creator. In this tradition, a spiritual leader uses seven kinds
of wood to prepare three fires—two smaller fires set on either side
of a large central fire. The large fire represents the Creator and the
newlyweds. The smaller fires represent the lives of the bride and
groom before their wedding vows were exchanged. After tobacco,
sage, sweet grass and corn are sprinkled over the firewood, prayers
are said, songs are sung and then the wood piles are set aflame.
Once the fires are well established, the bride and groom slowly
push their small fires into the large central one, signifying their
union.

Step to It

Another significant use of fire occurs in a traditional Hindu
wedding ceremony. In the *Saptha Padhi* ritual, the bride and
groom join hands and take seven meaningful steps around a ceremonial fire. The following is then recited: "We have taken the
seven steps. You have become mine forever. Yes, we have become
partners. I have become yours. Hereafter, I cannot live without
you. Do not live without me. Let us share the joys. We are word
and meaning united. You are thought, and I am sound."

Step ON it

No, that heading does not refer to an eager bridezilla's instructions to her limo driver. Stepping on a wineglass at a Jewish ceremony is symbolic of the destruction of Jerusalem's First Temple. A more glass-half-full interpretation of the tradition is that the wine in the wineglass signifies life's prosperity and goodness, and the breaking of the glass represents disappointment. This teaches a young couple to appreciate what they have. Yet another less-orthodox explanation is that the gesture foreshadows the bride's loss of virginity. Similarly, a Japanese groom will crush an egg with his bare foot to demonstrate the fragility of marriage.

Aptitude for Food

Food, particularly bread, is frequently and ceremoniously woven into many ethnic weddings. In Germany, women carry a loaf of bread and some salt to attract wealth and good luck. An Egyptian bride might believe pinching bread will bring luck and fortune. Various foods incorporated into Nigerian wedding ceremonies are sampled by the bride and groom and then shared with guests. The foods might include honey and/or sugar to represent a sweet union. When the obi, or kola nut, is shared, it is often accompanied by the following phrases: *Won ma gbo. Won ma to. Won ma d'agba.* This translates as: They will ripen. They will not go hungry. They will grow old.

Sweet as Honey

Although a woman shouldn't have to play hard to get (à la *The Rules*) once she has the ring, in this Iranian wedding custom, playing hard to get is endearing. During the ceremony, the groom asks his bride three times to say yes. The first two times, she coyly avoids answering. Finally, she says yes, and the bride and groom dip their little fingers into a glass of honey and bring it to the other's mouth. Now the groom may kiss the bride.

Rice—It's Not Just for Confetti

In a traditional Korean wedding, the bride and groom share three spoonfuls of rice, a gesture signifying their intention to share the rest of their lives together. A Korean rice liquor is then poured into two cups and presented to the couple. The bride and groom, in turn, pour their portions into a single cup that they will share, to signify the union of their souls.

Follow the Lanterns

In ancient Korea, hand lanterns were placed along the path to the bride's home the night before the wedding. The groom followed the lanterns, and the ceremony took place in the bride's house or yard. For the getaway, the happy couple was whisked away in a palanquin or cart. A chest of gifts was offered by the groom's family, with whom the newlyweds usually lived.

The Strength of Three

Greek wedding ceremonies are typically rife with religious symbolism. In one interesting Greek tradition, which takes place after the bride and groom have completed their wedding vows and are husband and wife, the couple walks around the church altar three times. The custom represents the Holy Trinity: God the Father, God the Son and God the Holy Spirit.

The Algonquin Wedding

Marriage is taken very seriously in the Algonquin tradition. The pipe carrier, who oversees the ceremony, must satisfy himself that the young man and woman wanting to marry are serious about their intentions. The Algonquin people do not recognize divorce, so if the pipe carrier has any doubts about the readiness of the couple, he can refuse to perform the ceremony. If he chooses to perform the ceremony, he will have the couple declare their intentions, then have each of them smoke from the ceremonial pipe. The pipe carrier then takes his turn, sealing the new couple's commitment.

A Saudi Wedding

There is much preparation leading up to a traditional Saudi wedding, but the ceremony itself does not take place in a mosque. Instead, the contractual part of the wedding takes place in a civil office several days before the wedding celebration. The bride and groom come before an Islamic magistrate, or sheikh, and three people, either three men or two women and a man, join the couple and the magistrate to witness the formalities.

For All Eternity

During a traditional Hispanic wedding ceremony, a priest blesses 13 gold coins that represent the groom's dowry to his bride. Another Hispanic tradition is to shape a figure-eight symbol around the shoulders of the bride and groom with a large rosary or rope. The figure eight symbolizes the eternal nature of their union. At the reception, guests often hold hands and surround the newlyweds in the shape of a heart during the first dance.

Eloping

According to Merriam-Webster's online dictionary, the word "elope" can be traced back to 1628; its etymology is based on the Anglo-French words *aloper* or *esloper*, meaning to abduct or run away. The actual practice of eloping seems to have originated in England. Under the Marriage Act of 1753, a marriage was only legal if the couple had their "banns of marriage" read in church on three consecutive Sundays prior to their wedding day. The banns publicly announced the couple's intentions and were put in place to ensure the marriage was on the up-and-up—that neither had another spouse hidden away somewhere, for example. The public announcement was also a way to inform others of the upcoming event, just in case they were opposed to the union and anxious to stop it. With such a public proclamation, it was tough for young folks in love to pull the wool over their parents' eyes, as it were. Hence, it became necessary, at times, to run off to another jurisdiction in which the practice was not in place—to Gretna Green in Scotland, for example.

"I wanna make you smile whenever you're sad...Carry you around when your arthritis is bad...All I wanna do...is grow old with you."

–Robbie (Adam Sandler), *The Wedding Singer* (1998)

VOWS AND PRAYERS

In addition to the traditional religious vows and personal vows written by and exchanged between the bride and groom is a plethora of vows and prayers unique to different cultural traditions and handed down through the ages. Although the following words might have been penned centuries earlier, their sentiments are as valid today as they were then.

Wedding Prayer

Lord, behold our family here assembled.
We thank you for this place in which we dwell,
For the love that unites us,
For the peace accorded us this day,
For the hope with which we expect the morrow,
For the health, the work, the food,
And the bright skies that make our lives delightful;
For our friends in all parts of the earth.
Amen.

–Robert Louis Stevenson (1850–94)

Something to Think About

In a traditional Taoist ceremony, the Prayer for Peace is recited.

If there is to be peace in the world,
There must be peace in the nations.
If there is to be peace in the nations,
There must be peace in the cities.
If there is to be peace in the cities,
There must be peace between neighbors.
If there is to be peace between neighbors,
There must be peace in the home.
If there is to be peace in the home,
There must be peace in the heart.

My Love, My Heart

This is one way the Inuit share their wedding vows.

You are my husband/You are my wife
My feet shall run because of you.
My feet dance because of you.
My eyes see because of you.
My mind thinks because of you.
And I shall love because of you.

Traditional Blessing

The Irish certainly have a way with words. The Irish Marriage Blessing is simple but profound.

May God be with you and bless you;
May you see your children's children.
May you be poor in misfortune,
Rich in blessings,
May you know nothing but happiness.
From this day forward.

Sweet and Strong

The *I Ching* reflects on the vows of marriage this way—a wonderful excerpt to use as a wedding toast.

When two people are at one in their inmost hearts,
They shatter even the strength of iron or bronze.
And when two people understand each other
In their inmost hearts,
Their words are sweet and strong,
Like the fragrance of orchids.

A Buddhist Prayer

May all beings be filled with loving kindness.
May they be well.
May they be peaceful and at ease.
May they be happy.

POST-CEREMONY TRADITIONS

What a couple does immediately after being pronounced husband and wife is often just as important as all they did to prepare for the big ceremony.

Steeped in Symbolism

A traditional Czech wedding overflows with symbolism. From the testing of the bride and groom to the final toast, every action holds a deeper meaning.

☛ At some time near the wedding date, the bride's friends might gather to plant a tree in her yard. The tree, decorated with ribbons and colored eggshells, is a sign of a new beginning. It is in the bride's best interest to take mighty good care of that tree—legend has it that if the tree dies, so will the bride.

☛ After the bride and groom have said their "I do's," wedding guests form a "wedding guard of honor" by standing as close to one another as possible, forming a solid wall of people for the bride and groom to walk through. These guests make it as tough as possible for the new husband and wife to make their way down the aisle. This exercise demonstrates the need to work together to overcome future hardships.

☛ At one point during the wedding reception, the bride and groom sit or stand together and a plate is smashed at their feet. They are expected to clean up the mess together, symbolizing unity in their marriage.

☞ Another lesson drilled home to the newlywed couple is one of trust. The couple is wrapped in a single towel and given a single spoon with which to eat a bowl of soup. The bride and groom must share the spoon and consume the soup together. This action is a sign of trust and a demonstration of the importance of being there for one another, especially during difficult times in the marriage.

Thank You and Go Procreate

A diverse assortment of gestures and offerings has been integrated into various cultural ceremonies as a way of saying thanks or good luck. A pine tree might be planted outside the home of Dutch newlyweds to bring luck and fertility. In Islam, eggs are symbols of fertility. Muslim newlyweds can be given a gift of eggs as they "eggs-it" the ceremony.

Asian Fusion

As a show of respect and gratitude, Japanese couples present their parents with sake; the bride and groom first sip from three cups, then present one each to the parents. The Chinese perform a similar ritual with tea.

Nut Grabbing

In Korean tradition, dates and chestnuts are indicators of off-spring, so the bride presents them as gifts to her new in-laws. In return, the nuts are tossed back to the bride, who turns the skirt of her bridal gown into a makeshift nut sack and tries to catch as many as she can.

More Nuts

A gift to a Greek bride and groom can include walnuts. This is because, as well as being a great source of important omega-3 fatty acids, walnuts break into four parts. The parts represent the bride, the groom and each of their families.

Seedy Superstition

In Nigeria, the fruit of the local *ata-ire* plant is opened; it is believed that the number of seeds inside indicates how many children the couple will produce.

Hazing of the Bride?

The Maasai people of Kenya have a most unusual way of show-ing their affection for the bride. It is customary for the father of the groom to bless the bride by spitting on her hands and breasts! The women might also get involved by insulting the bride to ward off evil spirits.

Pin the Money on the Bride

To create a substantial nest egg for the new couple, Filipinos employ a wedding custom referred to as "pinning the bride." As the name suggests, the guests physically pin money onto the bride's dress. The front of the bride's gown is for her family and guests; the backside is assigned to the groom's gang. Sometimes the custom escalates into quite the competition to see which side is the most pinned.

Showering of the Confetti

The idea of showering the bride and groom with confetti—the "throw," as it has come to be known—is actually a tradition of pagan origin, although what actually constituted "confetti" varied from age to age and culture to culture. Initially, bits of grain were thrown at a newly married couple, an act meant to wish them a fruitful union. The fertility of the seeds was thought to have an effect on the newlyweds, both in the harvest field and in the wedding bed!

I Want Candy

While the word "confetti" brings to mind small colored bits of paper, the term hearkens back to 1815 and the Italian word *confetto,* or "sweetmeat"—small candies tossed out to crowds gathered at carnivals and other festivals. The idea of throwing confetti is thought to have been adopted by the English, who converted the candy into the bits of colored paper.

What Else Can You Throw?

Confetti came in all manner of shapes and sizes, depending on what was most commonly available in any given country. Seeds and nuts often replaced wheat and other grains. (Apparently, a groom in the early Roman Empire made a habit of presenting his friends with walnuts or other available nuts at his wedding, signifying an end to his single days.) In Czechoslovakia, peas were commonly used to shower the newlyweds coming out of the church; Moroccans traditionally toss figs, dates or raisins; and candies and flowers were once the confetti of choice in Portuguese weddings.

More Uncustomary Confetti

☞ Red seems to be a popular color for luck. One Mexican tradition has friends and family tossing red beads at the new couple for just that reason—to wish them luck!

☞ Believe it or not, being pelted with eggs is common in some European countries. This is said to signify the new life into which the newlyweds are entering.

☛ One old Irish tradition offers a variation on the throw—the newlyweds are pelted with pots and pans, gently, of course. The pots and pans symbolize domesticity.

☛ Tossing birdseed is a modern response to an urban legend that suggests tossing rice is dangerous to birds. Another is the tossing of flower petals.

☛ And finally, for those of you who are determined to toss something at your newly married friends but don't want to have the wedding party charged with extra cleanup, consider blowing bubbles! It's apparently all the rage these days!

DID YOU KNOW?

Throwing rice was made popular in America, but its use stems much farther back than the modern world. Rice, in some cultures, was thrown to feed the evil spirits that might be planning to disrupt the ceremonies. Rice, along with other grains, was also viewed as a sign of fertility.

Go Ahead, Feed the Birds

Many folks believe throwing rice at a newly married couple as they leave the church can be potentially deadly to birds that later snap up the grains and eat them. They could not be more mistaken. This popular myth was exposed in 1996, after a newspaper article by noted columnist Ann Landers begged readers to "throw rose petals instead of rice. Rice is not good for the birds." Not wanting rice to get a bad wrap, the USA Rice Federation in Houston responded by saying the myth was just that, a myth. In her response, rice expert Mary Jo Cheesman pointed out that ducks and geese feed on rice while crops are still in the field, and "uncooked, milled rice is no more harmful to birds than rice in the field." So, if you're afraid a pigeon might explode after your relatives get a little carried away tossing rice, you can rest easy on that account. You might, however, want to make sure your guests are wearing sensible, slip-proof shoes.

Snagging the Shoes

Ever wonder where the practice of tying shoes to the bumper of the newlyweds' getaway car came from? According to one source, it all started with the bride's father. Legend has it that the father absconded with the bride's shoes and handed them over to her new husband as a symbol of passing authority over the woman from one to the other. (This apparently prevented the bride from running away.) Worse, the new husband would then tap his bride on the head, as if driving the significance of this act home to her. Although, today, the custom in its entirety could amount to nothing short of a mutiny, it is still quite common to see a wedding car scooting down the highway, with shoes or cans or other odd objects attached to its bumper.

Honk! Honk!

The tradition of honking the car horn after the wedding ceremony to announce the newlyweds to the world actually originated as yet another method of protecting the young bride from evil. Like braiding herbs into the bride's hair and dressing the bridesmaid like the bride, ringing loud bells or setting off firecrackers while escorting the bride from the wedding ceremony was an effort to scare away evil spirits. After all, you wouldn't want anything to put a crimp into the wedding-night festivities, would you?

One Long Day

It was once a Portuguese custom for the new couple to visit each of their guests at home the day after the wedding and personally thank them for attending. For obvious practical reasons, that tradition has been abandoned. Sending a nice card is now sufficient.

"Marrying my husband was no mistake. I had my reason, only I can't remember what it is."

–Jadzia Pzoniak (Lena Olin), Polish Wedding (1998)

EAT, DRINK AND BE MERRY

Today, 38 percent of weddings include a buffet, 34 percent have a sit-down dinner and 28 percent serve only cake and beverages. In weddings past and present, food has always played an integral part in the festivities.

Feasting it Up, Chinese Style

You had better have a flexible palate if you are planning to attend a traditional Chinese wedding. A feast in this tradition is not made up of what we know as Chinese food. Instead, it is loaded with dishes chosen primarily for their symbolism. Peking duck is a good example. It is one of the main courses and is often served with chicken and lobster. This juxtaposition or pairing of dishes is said to represent a yin-yang kind of balance between the male and female components of the new union. For example, the Chinese often refer to lobster as "dragon shrimp." Chicken represents "phoenix" and, when cooked in red oil, symbolizes a hope for prosperity. One source explains that "the dragon and the phoenix are hormones together, and the yin and yang elements in this family is balanced."

Also a popular dish at a traditional Chinese reception is sea cucumber, because it is believed to symbolize the harmonious union between the new bride and groom and a future without conflict. If you are invited to a Chinese wedding, bring your appetite—there are usually eight courses at a Chinese feast because the number is believed to be lucky.

DID YOU  KNOW?

A traditional Italian wedding feast must include the following good-luck foods: Italian wedding candy and fried dough shaped into bowties and sprinkled with icing sugar.

DID YOU  KNOW?

Kai fish, the "traditional fish of happiness," is a main menu item at most traditional Japanese receptions.

The Proof is in the Pudding

In a traditional Navajo wedding, the groom's family grinds white maize (corn), and the bride's family is responsible for contributing ground yellow maize. The two types are combined to create a pudding, which is first tasted by the bride and groom at their wedding reception.

Goodbye Chocolate Fountain

The hottest wedding dessert trend is the Candy Buffet. Fill large glass or plastic containers with jellybeans, gummy bears, hard candy and taffy, and let guests scoop the sweet-tooth fodder into dainty little sacks. Make sure to coordinate the sacks and ribbons with your wedding colors!

"What do you mean, he don't eat no meat?... Oh, that's okay. I make lamb."

–Aunt Voula (Andrea Martin), *My Big Fat Greek Wedding* (2002)

LET THEM EAT CAKE!

The tradition of having a special cake for the wedding reception dates back at least to the days of the Roman Empire, when the groom ate a portion of the cake and broke the remaining portion over the bride's head after the ceremony. This symbolized his dominance over her and the loss of her virginity. Guests scrambled to get a piece of the cake, believing it to bring them good luck. The Romans also believed that the act of the bride and groom feeding each other cake formed a magical bond.

A Tall Order

An unknown baker first contrived the wedding cake we know today sometime during the Middle Ages. In those days, it was customary for a new couple to kiss over a tall pile of buns or mini-cakes brought to the wedding reception by the guests. The successful completion of the kiss was thought to symbolize a prosperous future or lots of children—interpretations varied. The unknown baker in question came up with the idea of turning the pile of small cakes into one large cake. The idea took off, and, ever since, newlyweds everywhere have celebrated their weddings with the customary tiered wedding cake.

Bride's Pie

Although the idea of having a large wedding cake was catching on in more affluent circles, folks of more modest means celebrated their big day with a bride's pie. The practice originated sometime in the mid-1800s and continued for almost two centuries. The pie was filled with anything from sweetbreads to plain old mutton. However, hidden inside the filling was a much-coveted glass ring. The tradition dictates that the lucky lady to find the ring would be celebrating her own wedding next.

Cutting the Cake

Originally, it was the bride's job to cut the wedding cake for her guests, but as the numbers of guests grew, so did the size of the cake. Eventually, it became clear that the bride needed a little help if she was to cut a slice for all her guests and still have a little time leftover to mingle with them, too. That was when the groom jumped on board, and it became customary for the newlyweds to share the job. Symbolically, cutting the cake became the first duty the couple performed together. The groom placing his hand over his bride's signified his responsibility to take care of her.

The Groom's Cake

Although not much is known about this tradition (perhaps it's a conspiracy by some bakers' association to double their business), at some point in American history, it became fashionable for a wedding reception to include two cakes—the wedding cake and the groom's cake. Although the wedding cake was usually white, symbolizing the bride's virginity, the groom's cake was often chocolate. In one explanation for this two-cake tradition, the groom cut up his special cake and fed it to the bridesmaids. Another tells of the groom slicing and boxing pieces of his cake and handing it out to all the single women at the wedding. They, in turn, take the cake home and sleep with it under their pillows that night. The superstitious believed the young women would dream of their future husbands. This tradition is thought to have originated in the Old South.

Cake Déjà vu

The top tier of a wedding cake is often saved and frozen before being eaten by the bride and groom on their first anniversary. It is believed that if the cake lasts the first year, the marriage will be a long and happy one.

An Italian Flair

In some parts of Italy, a wedding cake as we know it is not served. In its place, guests are given a small but fancy gift bag or box filled with sugarcoated almonds. The treat is said to symbolize a wedding as being the "union of bitter and sweet."

Now That's Teamwork

The dried-apple-stack cake is a tradition rooted in the Appalachian Mountains area of the eastern United States. In this tradition, each of the couple's friends brings the future bride a thin layer of cake, which looks a little like a thick pancake. The bride layers the cake slices with apple preserves, apple butter, and dried apples. She continues to layer the cakes as they are presented to her until she receives the last cake. The popularity of the couple is assessed by the number of layers in the cake.

Leave it to the Irish

A traditional Irish wedding cake is the Irish Whiskey Cake. It's made up of a series of tiers and is crowned with a dose of good old Irish whiskey, in the form of a buttery whiskey topping. The top tier is often frozen and eaten during the festivities following the christening of the couple's first child or when the couple celebrates their first anniversary, whichever comes first.

DID YOU  KNOW?

Saint Bride's Church in London, England, is believed to be the inspiration behind the tiered wedding cake. If you have been to London and seen Saint Bride's many-tiered steeple, you understand why.

Pass the Bread

Instead of a wedding cake, the *korovai*, a large elaborate loaf of bread decorated with symbols and designs, holds the place of honor at the head table of a Ukrainian wedding. In the Ukrainian tradition, bread symbolizes the life-giving powers of the Sun and nature and also represents the "circle of life." Historically, how this bread was made was as important as the end product. An odd number of women (usually seven) gathered at the bride's home. Each contributed ingredients for the bread, bringing with her a cup of flour or an egg or water drawn from her own well, for example. The size of the bread, then, depended on the number of women involved in its production—the more participants, the greater the amount of ingredients, the larger the bread. The bread was mixed and kneaded while the women sang a ritual song, blessed before it was baked and then shared among the guests at the reception, to bring good luck and prosperity to the new couple.

In the same Ukrainian tradition, another smaller loaf of bread is presented to the new couple by their parents on their arrival at the reception. Salt and shots of vodka are also given to the bride and groom. This forms the formal blessing of the new couple. Today, although many Ukrainian families have adopted both bread traditions, they're not likely to adhere strictly to the traditional production of the bread. In fact, there are folks out there who make their living baking this bread for Ukrainian weddings.

Other Bread Customs

☞ In the Polish version of the bread tradition, the newlyweds are presented with bread, wine and salt: bread so they will always have enough food; salt to remind them that ups and downs are a part of life; and wine to represent health and happiness.

☞ The Russians added yet another dimension to the bread tradition. It is customary for the Russian bride and groom to bite into a loaf of homemade bread to ensure their health and prosperity. Legend has it that the spouse who bites the biggest piece of bread will rule the roost in that household.

☞ Norwegians also celebrate their traditional weddings with wedding bread, instead of wedding cake. The *brudlaupskling*, or wedding bread, was considered an exceptional delicacy, because white bread was at one time a rare commodity in that country. Cream, syrup and cheese were used to top the brudlaupskling, and, as with wedding cake, the bread was then shared among the guests.

Time is of the Essence

You had better start baking if you want to create the perfect Jamaican wedding cake in time for the wedding. Also known as Black Cake, this specialty is a heavily fruited cake soaked in rum for an entire year.

Wedding Art?

A traditional Lithuanian wedding cake looks a lot like a miniature evergreen made of pastry, although it has also been described as also looking like a coral reef. The *shakotis* was historically baked over an open fire.

Bon Appetit

Dating back to medieval times, the *croquembouche* was typically served at traditional French weddings. This variation on the wedding cake is a cone-shaped tower made up of individual, bite-sized, cream-filled puff pastries. The tiny morsels can be piled on top of one another to form the cone shape or can simply be layered on a tiered serving dish. A drizzle of caramel usually finishes off this light but decadent sweet.

A Charming Tradition

In Peru, charms are attached to ribbons woven between layers of the traditional wedding cake. Each single gal gets to pull out one ribbon. Although a variety of charms can be claimed, one charm in particular—a ring—is the most coveted. The girl who manages to choose the ribbon with the ring charm is lucky, indeed. Legend has it that she will be heading to the altar before the year is out.

Bad Luck Charm

A southern U.S. variation of the Peruvian wedding cake tradition is a little more ominous, at least, where the charms are concerned. In this tradition, good luck charms can predict everything from future children to travel; bad luck charms, however, can also be attached to the ribbons. It is all meant for a laugh, of course, but if you have superstitious friends, you might want to think twice before you follow this old practice, so stick to using the good charms only.

DID YOU KNOW?

In Nigeria, wedding cakes are often baked in the shape of the Bible or Quran.

You May Cut the Bride

One bride's dream is another bride's nightmare. Chidi Ogbuta made headlines with her truly one-of-a-kind wedding cake. Presumably a big Barbie doll fan, Ogbuta requested that the cake for her big day be a life-size replica of none other than herself! Nikki Jackson, of the Texas bakery Absolutely Edible Cakes, created the 5'4" (160-centimeter) dessert. Jackson claims she had to remove the doorframe to get it out of the bakery!

Creative Cakes

Buttercream, three tiers and cascading flowers are making way for Krispy Kremes, Lego toys and edible art. More and more modern couples are using the cake as an expression of their personalities and passions. Along with the aforementioned cakes made entirely of Krispy Kreme doughnuts and Lego building blocks have been cakes dedicated to everything from the Super Mario Brothers to UFOs and sports teams. Don't ignore the many opportunities for unique toppers. From Ken and Barbie to Morticia and Gomez Addams, the topper can become the true icing on the cake.

DID YOU  KNOW?

Breaking dishes sounds like it might be unlucky, but at least one old English custom makes it a necessity—when it comes to judging a new bride's future happiness, that is. On the bride's first visit home after the wedding, she is encouraged to put a piece of her wedding cake on a plate and throw it out a window. If the plate shatters, the news is good—she can look forward to a long and happy marriage. If the plate does not break, the omens are not good, strange as that might seem.

> *My customers' ideas on the subject are often perfectly crazy, and if I try to follow their instructions I am sure to turn out a real freak confectionery, and that is painful to professional pride.*

–a wedding-cake baker in "Strange Superstitions Concerned with Wedding Cakes," an article published in the *New York Times* in 1914.

KICKING UP YOUR HEELS

Every celebration needs good food and good music. Once those vows are uttered, it's time to kick up your heels and dance!

Dancing the Rjadovyj

In traditional Eastern Slovakian, Lemko and Carpatho-Rusyn weddings, the last dance before the bride and groom leave the reception for the night is called the *Rjadovyj* (also *Redovy* or *Radovy*), the Bridal Dance. In a typically large wedding, as is often the case in these cultures, the bride has her work cut out for her, because she is expected to take a turn on the dance floor with every guest vying for the privilege. The scene looks something like this: the guests form a reception line, which begins with the bride. The Rjadovyj is playing. Each verse is about 20 seconds long and refers to the family and wedding scene. Because friends and family can tailor the verses to suit the couple they are celebrating, the number of verses is potentially endless. Here are just a couple of the traditional verses:

Play musicians, play for me.
Play musicians, play for me.
On my happy wedding day.
On my happy wedding day.
Put some money in the plate.
Put some money in the plate.
Let the whole family help out.
Let the whole family help out.

As the wedding guests make their way down the line, they drop gifts of money into a basket or other receptacle. The Master of Ceremonies, who oversees the entire matter, then allows each guest to take his or her dance with the bride. Of course, the bride usually only dances a few bars of music with each person before the emcee taps his or her shoulder and invites the next guest to take a turn. At the end of the line, the music fades as the bride and groom leave the reception. Overall, I would say that's one heck of a late-night workout!

Babushka Dance

Once a Ukrainian bride enters the reception hall, her mother parades her around the gathering and, after the bride has greeted all her guests, leads her to a chair placed in the middle of the room. The formal headwear she wore during the wedding ceremony is replaced by the simple cotton babushka, which is how this dance acquired its name. Once seated, the guests form a circle around the bride, and each takes his or her turn dancing with her. The groom, in this dance tradition, is actually the last person to dance with his bride. To acquire the honor, he will have had to fight his way through the crowd!

Apron Dance

Another variation of a Ukrainian first-dance tradition is the apron dance—and it appears to be a particularly lucrative dance, in terms of acquiring extra pocket change. In this tradition, the bride wraps an old apron around her waist, and the male guests take turns dancing with her. For the honor, they are expected to fill her apron pockets with money! The groom is not left out of this tradition, either. He makes his rounds with the ladies, while they drop their extra change into his pants pockets. If the bride's and groom's dance partners start competing, the newlyweds can come away with quite a significant haul!

Circular Dance

During a Czech wedding reception, the bride often takes part in the circular dance. The bride closes her eyes and dances, surrounded by a protective circle of men. The single girls attending the reception try to break through the wall of men, with the goal of ripping off a piece of the bride's veil. Eventually, someone breaks through the bride's bodyguards, which, in the Czech tradition, symbolizes the bride's loss of innocence and virginity.

Passing the Buck

The wedding song is played sometime after the halfway mark of the reception at Czech weddings. At this point, the groom removes the bride's veil. The veil—or the bride's or groom's shoes, or any combination of the three—is then passed around to all of the guests with the hope of collecting a little honeymoon money.

Dancing for your Dinner

The Spanish version of dancing for dough is called the *sequidillas manchegas*. In this tradition, however, the tables are turned. During the wedding reception, the bride and groom get to sit while the guests dance before the bride to entertain her and bring her gifts. Sometimes the newlyweds will also auction off her garter or pieces of his tie.

Hog's Trough Dance

Yes, it is as embarrassing as it sounds. Cajun wedding tradition deems it good luck for the bride and groom if their older siblings dance ("hog wild," if you will) in an empty hog trough until the trough breaks.

The Old Ball and Chain Dance

Here's something new. And you thought the Dollar Dance was humiliating! One up-and-coming reception shenanigan is the practice of forcing the poor groom to wear an eight-pound (3.5-kilogram) ball chained to his body. He spends the first half of the reception running…er, limping…from table to table, asking, "Do you have the key?" Many three-sheets-to-the-wind guests who have never heard of this modern trend have no idea what he's talking about, so he must take five minutes to explain: "Ha ha…this predicament…ha ha…it was my new father-in-law's idea…ha ha…seriously, do you have the frickin' key, or not?" When the groom finally stumbles across the guest entrusted with the key, he can remove the dead weight and…go bowling?

> Michael: "It is the duty of the best man to dance with the maid of honor."
>
> Julianne: "Dance? You can't dance. When did you learn how to dance?"
>
> Michael: "I've got moves you've never seen."
>
> –Julianne Potter (Julia Roberts) and Michael O'Neil (Dermot Mulroney), *My Best Friend's Wedding* (1997)

CHEERS!

Toasting the newly married couple is a common practice at most weddings, but it is a tradition that has evolved considerably from its early origins. The wedding toast is thought to have started out in 16th-century France, but it began as a means of recognizing someone in authority at a formal event. A piece of bread was placed at the bottom of a goblet, which was then filled with wine. This goblet was passed around among those gathered until it reached the guest of honor. He or she was then responsible for finishing the wine and consuming the bread. The custom was adapted for the wedding reception: the young couple hoisted goblets filled with wine and soggy bread and drank away until they had eaten the bread. It was believed that the person to finish first would "rule the household!"

Blending Families

Another popular French wine tradition saluted the merging of two families. This was accomplished by providing the bride and groom with glasses of wine, each from a different vineyard. The newlyweds poured the wine from their respective goblets into a third glass and shared the blended drink. This symbolized the uniting of the couple, as well as the blending of the two extended families.

Coupe de Marriage

Another French wedding tradition involves a two-handled cup, which is passed from one family member to another. The couple toasts each other using this cup, called a *coupe de marriage*.

DID YOU  KNOW?

A traditional Italian toast to the bride and groom is, *"Evviva gli sposi!"*—"Hurray for the newlyweds!"

So Much for the Glasses

Russians encourage a little mischief at their traditional weddings. Once guests and the bridal party finish their champagne, they slam their fluted glasses onto the floor. Notwithstanding the obvious mess, the shattering of these glasses is a good sign—it means the newlyweds can expect a happy marriage.

A Way with Words

The Irish are certainly a loquacious lot, especially when it comes to toasting a new bride and groom. There are more than a dozen popular Irish wedding toasts. Here is one for the road:

May your neighbors respect you, trouble neglect you,
the angels protect you, and heaven accept you.
May the Irish hills caress you.
May her lakes and rivers bless you.
May the luck of the Irish enfold you.
May the blessings of Saint Patrick behold you.

Others Say It This Way

☛ The Chinese say "*Ganbei*" and the Japanese say "*Kanpai*." Both mean "dry your cup."

☛ The Germans say "*Prost!*"; the Dutch toast "*Proost!*"; the English just say "Cheers."

☛ Other traditions toast to health: French (*Santé*), Irish (*Sláinte*), Italian (*Salute*), Spanish (*Salud*), Russian (*Vashe zdorovie*), and Welsh (*Iechyd da*).

☛ The traditional Hebrew toast, "*Le'chaim*," means "to life."

☛ Another popular Italian toast is "*Per cent'anni*"—"for one hundred years."

☛ There are at least two popular toasts in the Polish tradition: "*Sto lat*," which is a wish for a hundred years of happiness for the young couple, and "*Na zdrowie*," which is a wish for good health.

What Not To Say

The big toasts can make or break a reception. The following priceless (and tasteless) remarks are attributed to Brian Webster, the best man at his brother's wedding. What garnered a few chuckles at first evolved as the speech went on, resulting in uncomfortable tension and one furious bride. And poor Uncle Frank....

☛ "Being a best man is like making love to Queen Elizabeth. Sure, it's an honor, but nobody wants to do it."

☛ "The only thing tighter than his [the groom's] morals is his underwear."

☛ "We're talking about a guy who would only agree to have a stripper at his bachelor party if she was Christian."

☞ "Their love is as certain as the destruction of Uncle Frank's liver."

☞ "Their love is as sure as Uncle Frank's need for Viagra."

Groom Ed evidently retaliated by posting a video of the toast on YouTube, along with the message, "You will marry someday, Brian. Lest I not forget." Though I wouldn't bet money on Brian finding somebody to marry him....

Raise a Glass, Not an Eyebrow

A good best man toast should generally avoid touching on the subjects of former boyfriends or girlfriends, prior marriages, the cost of the wedding, secrets or confidential matters (especially medical or legal disclosures) and anything related to the honeymoon activities, with the possible exception of the location.

Other regrettable lines from actual wedding toasts:

☞ "You will be a great husband, but not as great as that stripper from last night. I can't believe that your mother-in-law can move like that...."

☞ "Congratulations on the termination of your isolation, and may I express an appreciation of your determination to end the desperation and frustration which has caused you so much consternation, in giving you the inspiration to make a combination to bring an accumulation to the population."

☞ When Ivana Trump married her fourth husband in 2008, her son stepped up to the microphone with some choice words. Along with referencing his mother's "great boobs," Trump Jr. also made a point of mentioning, "We are a construction company, and we have job sites, we lose people. You better treat her right, because I have a .45 and a shovel."

☞ "And doesn't the bride look beautiful? That gown is exquisite. It must have cost a fortune...all that extra material." (OK, this last one is from a cartoon, not an actual wedding. But all of the others are real!)

"This is only the second time I've been a best man. I hope I did OK that time. The couple in question are at least still talking to me. Unfortunately, they're not actually talking to each other. The divorce came through a couple of months ago. But I'm assured it had absolutely nothing to do with me. Paula knew Piers had slept with her sister before I mentioned it in the speech. The fact that he'd slept with her mother came as a surprise, but I think was incidental to the nightmare of recrimination and violence that became their two-day marriage. Anyway, enough of that."

–Charles (Hugh Grant), *Four Weddings and a Funeral* (1994)

WHEN THE PARTY'S OVER

Everyone knows that at some point during most receptions, the bride gathers all the young unmarried women around her and tosses her bouquet over her head into the throng of excited women. What's behind this quirky tradition? Maybe, just maybe, it has something to do with the wedding night....

A Great Escape

According to some sources, the bouquet-throwing tradition started as a way to distract the madding crowd gathering around the bride with the hope of ripping off a piece of her clothing. As far back as Roman times, folks gathered at a wedding believed that capturing something from the bride was good luck, because a bride on her wedding day was thought to be very lucky indeed. In fact, the bride was quite lucky to escape with any clothes on at all, so, to thin out the throngs of people grabbing at her dress, she started throwing her bouquet. While the vast majority of people turned their attention to the bouquet, the bride would escape relatively intact.

Up and Over

There are several theories about how the practice of carrying the bride over the threshold originated. One suggests that it ensured good luck for the newly married couple. According to another, the tradition developed at a time when it was considered appropriate for the bride to look a little uneasy about "giving herself" to her new husband, if you know what I mean. Yet another theory has the practice of carrying the bride over the threshold originating in Roman times, when the groom's friends lifted her over. This was to ensure the bride did not slip and fall, which was considered a very bad sign, indeed. All of these theories are preferable to the one that suggests that grooms kidnapped their wives and carried them over the threshold of their new home against their will.

Privacy Control

Throughout the ages, several cultures have used safeguards to ensure a marriage was indeed consummated on the wedding night. Sometimes, this meant having witnesses to the event. (Talk about pressure!) At some point during medieval times, the custom of tossing a garter into the rowdy crowd developed. The intention was to distract the voyeurs hoping to get a peek at the main event. The chap who caught the keepsake was considered a lucky man!

Intimate Puzzle

In preparation for her wedding, an Indian bride often has her hands hennaed. Hidden somewhere in the elaborate design is the groom's name. On the wedding night, the groom is charged with finding his name.

Disturbing the Peace

Newlyweds in the Middle Ages were customarily disturbed on the wedding night by friends, who used just about anything, including guns, to make noise throughout the night.

Marital Relations

In Saudi Arabia, it is customary for the groom's family to escort him to the room in which the newlyweds will consummate the marriage. The relatives visit over coffee and eventually leave. The bride's family then escorts her to the room, and the visiting continues a little longer, until they, too, leave. After that, there are no interruptions—at least, not planned ones!

Wrapped and Tied

Another ancient tradition finds the bride gift-wrapped in a bed sheet, secured by a knot tied in the front. This symbolizes that the bride is a virgin, and the groom gets to "untie the knot."

A Romp in the Hay

In one Celtic tradition, the bride and groom spend their wedding night in a barn. The bride is dressed and readied for her groom by her girlfriends, but before the groom catches a glimpse of his new wife, the male wedding guests have a chance to enter the barn and kiss the bride good night!

Knockin' Boots

An old Russian tradition deals with a few formalities before the newlyweds get down to the wedding-night fun stuff. Before the wedding, the bridegroom puts money into his boots. On the wedding night, the bride removes his boots as a sign of her intention to be obedient to her husband. He, in turn, hands over the money in his boots as a sign of his intention to provide for her. After this, the bride and groom are expected to consummate their marriage. If they fail to do so, superstition dictated that their union would not be a happy one.

DID YOU KNOW?

An old superstition common throughout Europe and parts of Asia states that if a bride falls asleep before her groom on their wedding night, she will die before he does.

Baby Luck

The preparation of the wedding bed is especially important in a traditional Greek wedding and entails an actual ceremony. Friends and family members make the bed with hand-knit linens and then scatter it with coins, rose petals and sugarcoated almonds, known as *koufetta*. It is also customary, whenever possible, to roll a baby on the marriage bed to encourage fertility.

Securing One's Fertility

The Irish believe that tying a laying hen to the couple's marriage bed will ensure fertility. The couple could avoid this noisy option, however, by simply eating a double-yoked egg! Fertility is also the reason behind the Scottish tradition of having a lactating woman prepare the couple's marriage bed.

Let Us In!

A newly married French couple could find their first night together a little busy—in more ways than one! It is tradition in that culture for friends to gather outside the newlyweds' window, banging pots and pans and singing loudly, until they are finally invited inside for food and drink!

DID YOU  KNOW?

According to one European study, 60 percent of couples do not consummate the marriage on their wedding night.

The Name Game

Here is an interesting wedding superstition that has been passed on, in rhyme, throughout the ages:

To change the name and not the letter
Is to change for the worse and not the better.

The moral of the story is that your man's last name had better start with a different letter than yours.

DID YOU  KNOW?

The most popular first name for a bride today is Jennifer; for grooms, it is Michael.

"Life after death is an improbable as sex after marriage."

–Mrs. White (Madeline Kahn), *Clue* (1985)

WEDDINGS WITH A PEDIGREE

Marie Antoinette's marriage to Louis XVI in 1770 represented more than the joining of two people. It symbolized the harmony between two nations. From the King of France to the King of Rock 'n' Roll, a royal wedding is no small affair.

Royal Revelations

Although wedded bliss is not what we automatically think of when reflecting on Britain's younger royals, Queen Elizabeth II has a lot to be thankful for in her own marriage. In November 2007, in celebration of the 60th wedding anniversary of Queen Elizabeth and Prince Philip, Buckingham Palace released "60 wedding facts" to the media—trivia tidbits about the longest royal marriage in British history. Here are some of the amazing highlights:

☛ No other British royal couple has managed to celebrate a 60th wedding anniversary. The young Princess Elizabeth was only eight years old when she first met her future betrothed, Philip. They were engaged on July 9, 1947, and married on November 20th of the same year.

☛ Philip was made Duke of Edinburgh by King George VI the day he and Elizabeth married.

☛ The royal couple was married at Westminster Abbey. It was the 10th time a member of the royal family was married there, the first having been the marriage of King Henry I to Princess Matilda of Scotland in 1100.

☞ Other royalty, including the King and Queen of Denmark, the King and Queen of Yugoslavia, the Kings of Norway and Romania and the Shah of Iran, joined the British couple in celebration of their special day.

☞ The silk used to make the Queen's wedding dress came from the hard work of thousands of Chinese silkworms at Lullingstone Castle.

☞ A total of 91 choristers, made up from the Abbey Choir, the Choir of HM Chapels Royal and others, huddled together in the organ loft to perform during the ceremony.

☞ It was following the signing of the register at this wedding that the trumpet fanfares were first sounded during a royal wedding.

☞ Among the more than 2500 wedding gifts bestowed on the happy couple was a piece of crocheted lace made from yarn spun by Mahatma Gandhi. It was inscribed "*Jai Hind,*" meaning "Victory for India."

☞ The wedding cake towered nine feet (2.8 meters) high and consisted of four tiers.

☞ Queen Elizabeth and Prince Philip have four children. Two children, Prince Charles and Princess Anne, were born before the Queen's coronation. The birth of Prince Andrew in 1960, some eight years after she was made queen, marked the first time since 1857, when Queen Victoria bore Princess Beatrice, that a reigning queen had given birth.

Hollywood Royalty

The royal Hollywood wedding of all time was the day the King
of Rock 'n' Roll said "I do." Elvis Presley and his princess,
Priscilla Ann Wagner (Beaulieu), tied the knot on May 1, 1967.
Elvis met the very young Priscilla in 1959, after her stepfather
was transferred and her family relocated to Wiesbaden, West
Germany. Elvis was on a tour of duty in Germany at the time,
and a mutual friend, U.S. Airman Currie Grant, introduced
him to Priscilla. Their immediate attraction to one another was
obvious, and for the next few months they continued to see
each other. Of course, love is one of the casualties of war; Elvis's
tour of duty ended and he returned Stateside, while Priscilla
remained with her family in Germany. But, although Priscilla
had been dubbed by the press as "the girl he left behind," the
couple corresponded by mail. Eventually, after a lot of begging
and pleading, Priscilla convinced her parents to allow her to
move into Graceland.

While Elvis was busy working, Priscilla finished her schooling. In her mind, the life that lay before her was not complete without Elvis. The couple had their struggles, however; Elvis had at least one affair before the couple married and several during their time together.

Presley Wedding Trivia

- ☞ Elvis and Priscilla married on May 1, 1967. Priscilla was almost 22 years old by then; she met Elvis when she was just 14, which means they dated for about seven years before exchanging wedding vows.

- ☞ The wedding was held in Milton Prell's suite at the original Aladdin Hotel in Las Vegas, with Nevada Supreme Court Chief Justice David Zenoff officiating. The Aladdin was demolished in 1998.

- ☞ The King wore a black tuxedo and cowboy boots. Priscilla wore a white gown with a tulle veil and a rhinestone crown.

- ☞ Priscilla's maid of honor was her sister, Michelle Beaulieu. Elvis had *two* best men: Joe Esposito and Marty Lacker.

- ☞ The civil ceremony was followed by a press conference and a breakfast reception. The newlyweds danced to "Love Me Tender."

- ☞ Priscilla was widely reputed to be a virgin when the couple married.

- ☞ The Presleys had a second wedding reception at Graceland on May 29, 1967.

- ☞ The couple welcomed their only child, Lisa Marie Presley, into the world on February 1, 1968, exactly nine months after their wedding night.

- ☞ The two Hollywood icons separated on February 23, 1972. Their divorce was finalized on October 9, 1973.

Elvis Marries Again

Different Elvis. Twice-divorced singer/songwriter Elvis Costello married Grammy-winning recording artist Diana Krall. The December 5, 2003, wedding was held just outside of London at Elton John's estate. One hundred and fifty guests, including Sir Paul McCartney, danced to music by the Irish band the Chieftains.

Hollywood Marries Royalty

Grace Kelly was known for acting in films such as *To Catch a Thief* and *Dial M for Murder*, but, on April 18, 1956, she took on a new role: Princess Grace of Monaco. Kelly and Prince Rainier of Monaco were first married in a civil ceremony, followed the next day by a religious ceremony, which was billed as the Wedding of the Century. Thirty million viewers watched on television as the couple exchanged vows at Saint Nicholas Cathedral in Monaco, and 700 guests attended the reception at the Palace Court of Honor. The bride's high-necked gown, a gift from MGM Studios, was made by famed designer Helen Rose and featured almost 150 yards (137 meters) of silk, taffeta and rose-point lace. The lace was said to have been more than 100 years old and purchased from a museum in Brussels. The groom wore a military-style Napoleonic uniform that he designed himself, and he used his sword when the pair cut the six-tiered wedding cake.

DID YOU  **KNOW?**

When Keely Shaye Smith became Brosnan, Mrs. Pierce Brosnan, in 2001, she wore a beaded Richard Tyler gown that was reportedly inspired by Princess Grace's wedding dress. Their wedding reception took place at the Ashford Castle hotel in Ireland, where Princess Grace once stayed, and they also had a six-tiered cake.

"A wedding is a sacrament...a joyous celebration of love and commitment. In Utopia. In the real world...it's an excuse to drink excessively and say things you shouldn't say."

–Nick Mercer (Dermot Mulroney), *The Wedding Date* (2005)

NUMEROUS NUPTIALS

The more the merrier…and, for some folks, that refers to number of spouses, too. Some celebrities simply cannot settle down.

Nirvana at Nine?

If there was an award given to the actress with the most "I do's" under her belt, that dubious honor would likely go to Zsa Zsa Gabor. The flamboyant Hungarian actress, who waltzed down the aisle a total of nine times, was born Sari Gabor on February 6, 1917, and said her first "I do" at the age of 20. That was when she married Turkish intellectual Burhan Belge. The couple divorced in 1941, and on April 10, 1942, Zsa Zsa married Conrad Hilton Sr. That marriage lasted until 1947, and Zsa Zsa did not remarry again until April 2, 1949, when she said her vows to English actor George Sanders. Ironically, their divorce was made final on their fifth anniversary, on April 2, 1954. She remained on the singles' circuit until November 5, 1962, when she married Herbert Hutner. They divorced on March 3, 1966. From there, Zsa Zsa went through a couple of shorter marriages: to Joshua S. Cosden Jr. (March 9, 1966 to October 18, 1967), and Jack Ryan (January 21, 1975 to August 1976). Her August 27, 1976 marriage to Michael O'Hara ended in divorce in 1982. However, something must have been off about that divorce, because Zsa Zsa's April 13, 1983, marriage to Felipe de Alba was annulled the next day on the grounds that her divorce from O'Hara was not properly settled. Finally, on August 14, 1986, Zsa Zsa appeared to find true love at last when she married Frederic Prinz von Anhalt. The couple is still married, as of this writing, but the relationship has not been without its controversy. On February 9, 2007, Prinz von Anhalt went public, claiming he fathered Anna Nicole Smith's baby girl, Dannielynn. He said he had been having an ongoing affair with Anna Nicole since the 1990s, but, even if that were true, a DNA test ruled him out as the baby's biological father in April of the same year.

Zsa Zsa's Views on Marriage

According to the Internet Movie Database biography on Ms. Gabor, Zsa Zsa is a woman of many quotes. Not surprisingly, for a woman who has married nine times, many of them have to do with her views on marriage. At the very least, they give you something to think about.

☛ A man in love is incomplete until he is married. Then he is finished.

☛ Husbands are like fires. They go out if unattended.

☛ I am a marvelous housekeeper. Every time I leave a man, I keep his house.

☛ A girl must marry for love, and keep on marrying until she finds it.

☛ Personally, I know nothing about sex because I've always been married.

☛ It's never as easy to keep your own spouse happy as it is to make someone else's spouse happy.

☛ I believe in large families; every woman should have at least three husbands.

☛ And finally, after being asked during an interview how many husbands she'd had, Zsa Zsa replied, "You mean other than my own?"

Eight and Counting

Born in 1932, Elizabeth Taylor—second in line for most-married Hollywood actress—first entered matrimonial bliss at the tender age of 18, when she married Conrad "Nicky" Hilton Jr. on May 6, 1950. The ink was barely dry on the paperwork when the couple divorced on January 29, 1951. Marriage number two, to Michael Wilding, took place on February 21, 1952. That union lasted a little longer—the couple had two sons together before they divorced on January 26, 1957. Taylor then married Michael Todd on February 2, 1957, and on August 7 of the same year welcomed daughter Elizabeth Frances (Liza) Todd into the world. Sadly, Michael was killed in a plane crash near Grants, New Mexico, on March 22, 1958. On May 12, 1959, Elizabeth married Eddie Fisher. She divorced him on March 6, 1964. Nine days later, on March 15, Liz married actor Richard Burton. This marriage was the longest of her eight marriages. She did not divorce Richard until June 26, 1974. She obviously had second thoughts, however, because the two married for a second time on October 10, 1975. In this case, twice was not a charm, and the couple divorced again on July 29, 1976. Husband number six was John Warner. Liz and John married on December 4, 1976, and divorced on November 7, 1982.

Liz stayed single for almost 10 years before she married for the eighth and final time. The lucky chap this go-round was Larry Fortensky, whom she met when both were in rehab at the Betty Ford Center. The couple married on October 6, 1991, and divorced on Halloween 1996. Is there another marriage on the horizon for Dame Elizabeth? In October 2006, her relationship with photographer Firooz Zahedi was scrutinized for wedding bell possibilities. According to the BBC, she denied any plans for a ninth marriage, saying Zahedi was an "old and dear friend."

Other Contenders for the Most-married Prize

☛ Lana Turner: eight husbands, from bandleader Artie Shaw (1) to nightclub performer Robert Dante (8).

☛ Larry King: seven marriages to six different women.

☛ Former Paramount Studios head Robert Evans: seven wives, including *Love Story* actress Ali McGraw and a one-week union to actress Catherine Oxenberg.

DID YOU  **KNOW?**

The record for the most monogamous marriages goes to former Baptist minister Glynn Scotty Wolf. In his 88 years of life, he tied the knot a whopping 29 times! He also holds the record for most divorces: 28. The shortest of his marriages lasted only 19 days; his longest was 7 years.

She's been married so many times, she has rice marks on her face.

–Henny Youngman, American comedian

CELEBRITY WEDDINGS

*No, celebrities really are not just like us—unless you, too, have
rented an entire castle for your wedding. Your flower budget is
probably also not in the five digits, nor is Elton John likely to
be on your guest list.*

Tom Cruise and Katie Holmes

He had her at "hello." Or at least, "Will you be my date to an
onslaught of premieres, have my baby and then marry me?" To
describe Tom Cruise's courtship of Katie Holmes as "whirlwind" is putting it mildly. Faster than he can flip a bottle while
doing the "hippie hippie shake" on a bar, Cruise had whisked
Holmes to Paris and proposed at the top of the Eiffel Tower.
Baby Suri arrived soon after. Fans fiercely hoped Holmes would
not succumb to postpartum depression—Cruise's denounce-
ment of psychiatry and meds for treating PPD was well publi-
cized. He believed that, like Rain Man buying underwear at
K-Mart, taking an antidepressant "sucks."

Katie Holmes, or "Kate," as she was renamed under Cruise control, married her "top gun" in November 2006. As she made
her way down the aisle, the bride was breathtaking in Armani.
No word, though, on whether the pianist played *Canon in D* or
the theme from *Mission Impossible*. According to an article on
cultnews.com, there were some unusual components to the
Scientology wedding. Read on—if you can handle the truth.

☛ Cruise's best man was none other than Scientology leader
David Miscavige. Famous guests who made the trek to Italy
for the nuptials included Scientology ambassadors John
Travolta and Kelly Preston, fellow open-minded religious
thinker Richard Gere (a fan of Buddhism), David and
Victoria Beckham, Will Smith and Jada Pinkett Smith,
Jennifer Lopez and Marc Anthony, Jim Carey and Jenny
McCarthy, and even Cruise's one-time *Endless Love* costar
(and aforementioned antidepressant nemesis), Brooke Shields.

☛ Noticeably absent from the Cruise wedding? Any reference to God, Jesus or the Bible. Instead of learning traditional biblical scripture, Scientologists who ascend to "Operating Thetan Level Three" are taught about "implanting" (which has a far different definition than the usual Hollywood use of the term), which is done through space alien technology. At "Operating Thetan Level Eight," Scientology members can become privy to anti-Christianity rhetoric. Not sure how that sits with Holmes' Catholic family. A War of the Worlds? Scientology weddings are not recognized by the Catholic Church, either, so take that.

☛ At one point, the minister solemnly asked Cruise, "And when she's older, do you keep her still?" Cruise replied, "I do." Evidently Cruise's former wives, Mimi Rogers and Nicole Kidman, were up a Dawson's Creek on the aging promise.

☛ Before the newly pronounced husband and wife presumably boarded the mothership to embark on their honeymoon, the minister officially permitted Cruise and Holmes to seal the deal with a kiss. By one account, the couple locked lips for not less than three minutes. Reportedly, one spectator actually cried out "stop!"

☛ During the reception, Cruise led a rowdy sing-along rendition of the Righteous Brothers' "You've Lost that Lovin' Feeling." This, of course, was an homage to the famous Kelly McGillis-wooing bar scene in *Top Gun*. Better that than a reenactment of "Old Time Rock and Roll" in his underwear.

The ARCs of Scientology

One unique characteristic of Scientology weddings is the emphasis on the ARC, an acronym for the three elements Scientology founder L. Ron Hubbard believed constituted Understanding. A is Affinity, R is Reality and C is Communication. Another distinction is the departure from typical wedding vows. Scientology ceremonies often refer to a marital "pact." The minister asks the bride and groom to "never close their eyes in sleep without healing any breach of understanding with communication."

David Beckham and Victoria Adams

When the impossibly good-looking soccer deity married his inhumanly skinny pop princess in 2005, it was beyond posh. Perhaps the wedding planning went something like this:

David: So tell me what you want.

Posh: I wanna invite 250 guests.

David: What you really, really want.

Posh: I wanna, I wanna, I wanna, I wanna rent out an entire Irish castle.

David: I could fancy that. Now let's go to the pub for some bangers and mash.

Posh: I'll just have a water.

Girl willpower, indeed. Perhaps Poshy was anticipating squeezing her bum into a very fitted gown. The bride wore a $100,000 strapless Vera Wang dress that featured a five-foot (1.5-meter) train and a couture corset that cinched her waist to about 18 inches (46 centimeters).

The event was practically a holiday in England. Naturally, the cream of the British crop was on the guest list. And, because if you wanna be my lover, you gotta get with my friends…of course, all the Spice Girls were in attendance. The couple went on to perform the hat trick of producing three adorable sons, Brooklyn, Romeo and Cruz.

DID YOU KNOW?

Never overly modest, the Beckhams reportedly topped their wedding cake with figurines of the couple entwined and nearly nude. The topper was only one of many less-than-shy displays for the twosome. David appeared in nothing but Armani underwear on a billboard outside of Macy's in San Francisco. For her part, Victoria posed in the buff for designer Marc Jacobs' skin-cancer-awareness T-shirts with the tagline "Protect the Skin You're In."

Elizabeth Hurley and Arun Nayar

When you can't decide where to marry, why not do it twice? In a 2007 union of Britain meets Bollywood, supermodel and actress Elizabeth Hurley and Indian businessman Arun Nayar first wed at Sudeley Castle in Winchcombe, England. The Friday civil ceremony was followed by a Saturday religious ceremony that featured a host of all-star guests: Donatella Versace (who designed the bride's dress); models Kate Moss, Elle Macpherson and Eva Herzigova; Prince Pavlos of Greece; Kate Winslet; Hurley's ex, Hugh Grant; and Elton John, who made a grand entrance via helicopter and gave away the bride at the ceremony. The bride and groom and about 60 guests were then whisked away in a $300,000 private jet to Mumbai, India, for a week of further celebrating. They reportedly exchanged vows again in a traditional *haldi* ceremony. This included the Indian custom of purifying the bride and groom by smearing them with a paste of turmeric, milk and cream. The festivities were also complete with elephants and fire eaters.

Madonna and Guy Ritchie

Just like Posh and Becks, Madonna and Guy Ritchie were considered by many to be British royalty, even though she's American (don't let the pseudo-aristocratic accent fool you). Also like the Beckhams, they decided to rent out an entire castle to ensure privacy for the occasion, an intimate affair at Skibo Castle in Scotland. Only about 60 guests witnessed the queen of reinvention marry the *Snatch* director in December 2000. However, those guests included Elton John (does this guy ever miss a wedding?), Sting, George Clooney, Brad Pitt and Gwyneth Paltrow. Always the Material Girl, Madonna and her then-hubby spent more than a million dollars on the elaborate fireworks, food and champagne. Unfortunately, the marriage has since crumbled, but back in happier times, it was the wedding of the year.

DID YOU  KNOW?

Actress Ashley Judd met her future husband, race-car-driver Dario Franchitti, at a 1999 wedding reception. The pair wed at Skibo Castle in Scotland and spent US$175,000 to rent all 40 rooms. A Scottish native, Franchitti wore the traditional kilt during the ceremony.

Wayne Gretzky and Janet Jones

From British celeb-royalty to the event known as Canada's Royal Wedding. In July 1988, hockey legend Wayne Gretzky married dancer and actress Janet Jones, who was expecting the first of their five children at the time. The million dollar-plus nuptials took place at Saint Joseph's Basilica in Edmonton and were televised throughout Canada. Interestingly, Alan Thicke, *Growing Pains* patriarch, hosted the reception.

Beyoncé and Jay-Z: Crazy in Love

April 4, 2008, was a monumentous date for "crazy in love" two-some Jay-Z (real name Sean Carter) and Beyoncé Knowles. They decided to tie the knot on 4/04 because the number four is of special significance to both. Each was born on the fourth: September 4 for Beyoncé; December 4 for Jay-Z. They also both have the Roman numeral IV tattooed on their ring fingers. Jay-Z even named his club 40/40, which is also a baseball term. The extravagant wedding took place at rapper-turned-mogul Jay-Z's New York apartment. Guests included Beyoncé's Destiny's Child gal pals Michelle Williams and Kelly Rowland and Coldplay lead singer Chris Martin and wife Gwyneth Paltrow. Underneath a great white tent, the rooftop party lasted well into dawn.

Donald Trump and Melania Knauss

Let's hope the third time is the charm for real estate mogul Donald Trump and Slovenian model Melania Knauss, 24 years his junior. Their wedding was charming, to say the least. The bride wore a satin Christian Dior Haute Couture gown, esti-mated to be worth between $100,000 and $200,000 and weigh-ing 50 pounds (22.5 kilograms)! The gown's 13-foot (4-meter) train was only upstaged by the 16-foot (5-meter) veil. The 30-minute ceremony at Palm Beach's Bethesda-by-the-Sea Episcopal Church was followed by a lavish reception in a ball-room trimmed with 24-carat gold at Trump's Mar-a-Lago Club. The 350-plus star-studded guests included Tony Bennett, Billy Joel, Rudy Giuliani, Hillary Clinton, Shaquille O'Neal, Barbara Walters, Don King, Katie Couric and Matt Lauer, and of course Trump's "eyes and ears" from *The Apprentice*, George H. Ross and Carolyn Kepcher.

Mad Money

Per usual, Trump spared no expense for his wedding; he spent $500,000 on flowers and $18,000 on caviar, and, at $650 a pop, bottles of Cristal flowed freely. By all accounts, everything went quite smoothly, and Trump didn't have to "fire" anyone. Though one group dared to say no to Mr. Trump. The Palm Beach town council rejected his request for a permit to launch fireworks at the reception. Guess who prevailed? At around 10:00 PM, a breathtaking fireworks display exploded in the sky.

Tiger Woods and Elin Nordegren

For a guy accustomed to dominating the leader board on the greens, it is no surprise that the Green Monkey golf course was part of the reception site when golf great Tiger Woods married Swedish model Elin Nordegren. Everything was on par as the lovebirds tied the knot in October 2004 during a beautiful sunset ceremony in St. James, Barbados. The event included a performance by Hootie and the Blowfish and was attended by about 120 guests, including sports legends-turned-frequent-celebrity-golf-tournament-contestants Michael Jordan and Charles Barkley. To ensure privacy from the paparazzi, Woods rented all 200 rooms of the luxurious Sandy Lane Beach resort. Staying on course with that theme, the couple honeymooned around the Caribbean on a 155-foot (46-meter) yacht appropriately named *Privacy*.

Score: Love All

From one athlete who finally met his match to another. Seven-time Wimbledon champ Pete Sampras first saw his future wife Bridgette Wilson on the screen in the ironically titled film *Love Stinks*. The movie might have stunk, too, but the tennis superstar was smitten with the model-turned-actress. He pursued her as if chasing down a lob from the net, and the two married in September 2000. Naturally, the reception took place inside a tent on a tennis court!

White Female, but No Longer Single

From Bridgette to Bridget. Just one week after a scary solo Malibu car crash that hospitalized actress Bridget Fonda with fractured vertebrae, things started looking up. It was announced that the never-before-married Fonda, 39 at the time, had become engaged to composer Danny Elfman. The two married in a candlelit ceremony at Los Angeles' First Congregational Church in November 2003. The bride walked down the aisle with her father, legendary actor Peter Fonda.

Secret Weddings

Most brides want to scream from the rooftops on their wedding day. But these very discreet couples decided to keep their marriages to themselves.

☛ Ben Affleck and Jennifer Garner—Perhaps Ben learned a lesson from the paparazzi-chronicled countdown to his doomed wedding to previous love Jennifer ("Jenny from the Block") Lopez. After all, when he married his *Daredevil* costar Garner, pregnant with their first child, in 2005 at the Parrot Cay resort in the Turks and Caicos, the ceremony was so intimate, not even their families and closest friends were in attendance. Garner's TV dad, Victor Garber of *Alias*, officiated the ceremony. No word on whether the famously stoic Jack Bristow cracked a smile after pronouncing them husband and wife.

☛ In another example of first-comes-love, then-comes-baby-carriage, *then*-comes-marriage, Affleck's ex, Gwyneth Paltrow, also shunned family for a super-secret, very private wedding in Santa Barbara in December 2003. The expectant mother-to-be and her Coldplay front man beau Chris Martin then fled to Cabo San Lucas for their honeymoon.

☛ Another preggers actress got hitched in an even more low-key manner. On May 19, 2008, Jessica Alba married Cash Warren in a Beverly Hills courthouse. The nuptials were so secretive, even Alba's own brother hadn't heard until he was interviewed by the press!

☛ Janet Jackson and Rene Elizondo—Jackson frequently collaborated with singer/songwriter Elizondo on many of her songs and videos. But very few people knew of their other collaboration—that they had been married since March 31, 1991! Taking secrets to another level, rumors have surfaced that Jackson has a "secret daughter," from her very brief marriage to James DeBarge when she was just 18 years old.

Till Death Do Us Part

Although marriage might be a fleeting endeavor in the often-fickle world of Hollywood, a number of celebrities have said, "I do" for the long haul and apparently meant it. Perhaps the most longstanding Hollywood marriage was that of the late Charlton Heston and his lovely wife, Lydia Marie Clark Heston. The couple married on March 17, 1944, and never looked back. For those not mathematically inclined, the Hestons celebrated 64 anniversaries together before Charlton passed away on April 5, 2008.

Other longstanding celebrity marriages of note:

☞ Tony Martin and Cyd Charisse, married on May 15, 1948. Although it was Tony's second marriage, the second one stuck until Cyd's death in 2008;

☞ James Garner and Lois Clarke, married on August 17, 1956;

☞ Alan and Arlene Alda, wed on March 15, 1957. They are still going strong more than half a century later;

☞ Joanne Woodward and the late Paul Newman, who celebrated their 50th wedding anniversary shortly before his death in September 2008. They married on January 29, 1958;

☞ Hal Linden and Francis Martin, wed on April 13, 1958.

Six Degrees of Happy Marriage Wisdom

Actor Kevin Bacon revealed to *OK!* magazine the secret to his successful marriage to actress Kyra Sedgwick. "All I know is the key to my marriage is just the fact that we like spending time together and we enjoy each other's company." A rare example of a Hollywood marriage with longevity, the couple has produced two children and celebrated their 20th wedding anniversary on September 4, 2008.

Actor Will Smith costarred with Tommy Lee Jones in *Men in Black* and its sequel *Men in Black II*. Tommy Lee Jones worked in Oliver Stone's *JFK* with none other than…Kevin Bacon! Will Smith was also featured in a film called *Six Degrees of Separation*. As for the trick to his marriage to actress Jada Pinkett Smith, which has been going strong for more than 10 years: "With Jada, I stood up in front of God and my family and said, 'till death us do part.' Divorce cannot be an option."

Sexiness wears thin after a while and beauty fades, but to be married to a man who makes you laugh every day, ah, now that's a real treat.

–Joanne Woodward, actress

FAMOUS MAY-DECEMBER MARRIAGES

George Bernard Shaw once said, "We don't stop playing because we grow old; we grow old because we stop playing!" Not a bad viewpoint, and Shaw lived to be 94 years old. Perhaps the individuals in May-December romances share a similar philosophy.

John and Cindy McCain

"By evening's end, I was in love," said McCain of meeting wife Cindy, 17 years his junior.

Fred and Jeri Thompson

The former Tennessee governor, presidential candidate and actor (to name a few of this busy guy's occupations) is 24 years older than his second wife, Jeri.

Woody Allen and Soon-Yi Previn

As if their 35-year age difference weren't controversial enough, Previn also happens to be the adopted daughter of Allen's former longtime lover, Mia Farrow. Farrow learned of their affair when she discovered nude photos of Previn among Allen's things. Yikes. Despite the scandal of their Italian wedding in 1997, they have beaten the odds by remaining together.

Speaking of Mia Farrow...

The actress and activist was entwined in her own May-December marriage when she wed Frank Sinatra, who was 29 years her senior.

Demi Moore and Ashton Kutcher

The gender tables were turned when this cougar married a cub 15 years her junior in 2005. In fact, Kutcher is only 10 years older than Demi's eldest daughter!

DID YOU KNOW?

Couples in general are waiting longer to take the plunge. The average age for first-time brides is 25. For first-time grooms, it's up to 27.5. The oldest bride on record is Australia's Minnie Munro. She was 102 years old when she tied the knot with a man almost 20 years younger!

Ivana Trump and Rossano Rubicondi

Another bolder older woman, the Donald's ex married an actor/model 20 years younger than her in 2008. Here's to you, Mrs. Robinson...er...Rubicondi....

Anna Nicole Smith and J. Howard Marshall II

Vickie Lynn Hogan, better known as *Playboy* centerfold and reality-TV star Anna Nicole Smith, was working at a topless bar when she met oil tycoon J. Howard Marshall II in 1991. In 1994, they married, despite their 64-year age difference and strenuous objections from Marshall's family. After Marshall's death in 1995, the late Anna Nicole spent years in court battling his son for control of his $1.6-billion estate.

Other Notable May-December Marriages

Hal Holbrook and Dixie Carter (14 years apart), Tommy Lee Jones and Dawn Laurel (18 years), Nicolas Cage and Alice Kim (20 years), Sofia Loren and the late Carlo Ponti (25 years), Christopher "Peter Brady" Knight and Adrienne "America's Next Top Model" Curry (24 years), Michael Douglas and Catherine Zeta-Jones (25 years), Chuck Norris and Gena O'Kelley (28 years), Clint Eastwood and Dina Ruiz (35 years), Tony Bennett and Susan Crow (33 years), Tony Curtis and Jill Vandenberg (45 years).

DID YOU  **KNOW?**

By most standards, there has to be at least an 11-year age gap to qualify as a May-December romance.

"I happen to believe in the sanctity of marriage, no matter how ugly or disgusting it gets."

–Frank Burns (Larry Linville) in *M*A*S*H*

WEDDINGS IN THE ERA OF TELEVISION

Part game show, part "reality" documentary, all IQ-lowering entertainment! Lord help us, it is not a new concept to seek love on public television. America breathlessly waited "two and two" to get right back to Love Connection's Chuck Woolery and his sympathetic puppy dogs eyes, as he listened intently to the disaster date of a woman with a bad perm and shoulder pads. The show seems downright quaint compared to the increasingly ridiculous and staged Blind Date or any of the generic MTV shows in which young monotone-script-reciting wannabes rarely bother feigning that it is love, not fame, they are seeking. People have also turned to television to test their love. Long before the so-hideous-you-can't-look-away unabashed trashiness of Temptation Island invaded living rooms, The Newlywed Game was inducing snickers with wink-wink innuendo as young brides were pinned between a rock and a hard place with personal questions.

The Bachelor/The Bachelorette

There have been many amazing journeys, and we have counted down several times to the most dramatic rose ceremony ever. But of all the years of *The Bachelor* and its spin-off, *The Bachelorette*, and all of the mind-numbing coupling combinations that could have resulted, there has only been one wedding. *Bachelor* season-one cast-off Trista Rehn got her own show and picked sensitive poet/firefighter Ryan Sutter to be her groom. In true met-through-reality-TV style, the couple accepted ABC's offer to televise their nuptials—as well as a behind-the-scenes wedding-planning special—in exchange for ABC forking over $4 million to foot their wedding bill and then some. All the while elevating the happy couple to reality-TV royalty.

Was the Theme Pepto Bismol?

In honor of the bride's favorite color, Trista and Ryan were flanked by pink bridesmaid dresses, pink chair covers, pink accents on the chocolate wedding cake and, to put their final rose ceremony to shame, more than 30,000 pink and ivory roses. Fans tuned in to see a Badgley Mischka-clad Trista exchange self-written vows with her teary-eyed new hubby.

Runner-up

After 11 seasons, *The Bachelor* has produced far more water-cooler conversation than marital bliss. But even if they have not yet marched down the aisle, one couplet from the show is at least still talking and, reportedly, even still dating. After Mary Delgado was dismissed by jolly Bachelor Bob Guiney in season four, it looked like she finally landed her big fish when she was chosen by professional fisherman Byron Velvick. That was before police were called to their home and Mary was arrested for alleged domestic violence against her man. So, one would assume he'd have tossed her back like a bad catfish, right? Well, despite her less-than-lovely mug shot, Delgado got Velnick to take her back. The couple remains committed...at least, as of press time.

So Close

Sarah Brice was selected as the final rose ceremony winner by actor Jerry O'Connell's less-eloquent little brother, Charlie O'Connell. While no Rebecca Romijn, Sarah had the good-girl/nurse thing going, and she and Charlie seemed to complement each other nicely. They still broke up, though only after a respectable two years together, and remain amicable, by all accounts.

Who Wants to Marry a Multi-Millionaire?

Women who had seen *Pretty Woman* one too many times lined up for *Who Wants to Marry a Multi-Millionaire*'s Mr. Rick Rockwell. In case you hadn't guessed, Rick Rockwell is not his birth name—did he see it in the opening credits of a porno and adopt it? Turns out that his name was not the only thing Rockwell misrepresented. He was not exactly the catch worthy of the beautiful gold diggers…er, women…lining up for him. Rockwell is a former *Star Search* loser, wannabe actor (the *Killer Tomatoes* movies) and mediocre stand-up comedian known for stealing material. It was also doubted that he warranted the "multi" prefix in his millionaire title. Oh, there was also the small business of a restraining order taken out against him by a former girlfriend he allegedly beat. Yes, quite the catch.

And then there's the shudder-inducing slobbery kiss with which he greeted his "winner." Rockwell opened his mouth like he was biting into a triple-decker club sandwich…or using the attacking mechanism of rabid tomatoes from outer space. Leggy blonde Darva Conger was as repulsed as the 22 million viewers at home. The honeymoon was over before it even started. Although they were married on the spot, Conger reportedly spent their honeymoon cruise sobbing and avoiding his advances like the plague. The marriage, which was never consummated, was annulled soon after.

Newlyweds: Nick & Jessica

Oh, Jessica. Not knowing whether it was chicken or tuna she was eating was the least of Ms. Simpson's problems. America watched Jessica's creepy stage father, Joe (commenting to the press about his daughter's cup size!), intrude on their lives. We watched Nick's career plummet—his first *SoulO* video looked like a low-budget remake of Gerardo's "Rico Suave." We watched Nick become increasingly exasperated by Jessica's helpless-ditz routine, and the marriage became a cautionary tale against marrying a girl who declares a virginity pledge to her father before puberty.

'Til Death Do Us Part: Carmen & Dave

They're both still alive. Obviously, Carmen Electra and Dave Navarro's "undying" love wasn't so…well, you get the picture. Maybe Dave got tired of Carmen spending all her time doing Aerobic Striptease and not including him. Or perhaps Carmen thought Dave borrowed her vixen gunmetal nail polish one too many times. Either way, their show aired one season; their marriage lasted only slightly longer.

My Fair Brady: We're Getting Married

When it's time to change, you've got to rearrange. That's what a voice-cracking adolescent Peter Brady sang on *The Brady Bunch*. The same goes for midlife-crisis Peter Brady. We thought all the Bradys had hit an all-time low with the shamelessly cheesy post-*Brady Bunch* variety show called *The Brady Hour*. Not even close. In this century, we've got Maureen (Marcia Brady) McCormick on VH1's *Celebrity Fit Club*. Barry (Greg Brady) Williams parodied Eminem's "The Real Slim Shady" with "The Real Greg Brady." (I'm Greg Brady, yes I'm the real Brady. All you other Greg Bradys are just imitating. So, won't the real Greg Brady please stand up….) Christopher (Peter Brady, after eating way too many pork chops and applesauce) Knight met America's Next Top Model Adrienne Curry when they ascended to the D-list on *The Surreal Life*. Shortly after, they decided to merge and form their own reality show chronicling their mismatched love-hate, real-fake mating rituals.

Farmer Wants a Wife

Ten city girls with names like Krista, Christa and Amanda compete for the heart of a hunky country…oh, who cares anymore?

"The only thing that holds a marriage together is the husband being big enough to step back and see where the wife is wrong."

–Archie Bunker (Carroll O'Connor) in *All in the Family*

DESTINATION WEDDINGS

If most of your wedding guests are shelling out travel expenses to attend your wedding, why not have them go somewhere exotic and fun? As opposed to, say, your current place of residence in Detroit or the small town (population 623) in which your fiancé grew up. Or perhaps it's family you want to escape from, by having an intimate wedding somewhere far away!

DID YOU  KNOW?

Twelve percent of weddings are considered destination weddings. The top destinations are:

- ☛ Las Vegas (more than 100,000 weddings per year)

- ☛ Hawaii (25,000 weddings per year)

- ☛ Bahamas (5000 weddings per year)

- ☛ Jamaica (5000 weddings per year)

- ☛ U.S. Virgin Islands (4000 weddings per year)

Other wedding destinations: About 2300 marriages a year are performed at Walt Disney World, and about 300 shopaholics exchange vows at the Wedding Chapel in Minnesota's Mall of America every year.

On Top of the World

Bride Moni Mulepati and groom Pem Dorjee scaled 29,035 feet (8850 meters) to get married. The Nepalese couple exchanged their vows atop Mount Everest in 2005, the first documented wedding at the world's highest peak. Their "wedding party" consisted of the other 45 climbers in the Rotary Centennial Everest Expedition. Treacherous weather conditions kept the ceremony brief, but the couple did take time to remove their oxygen masks and don celebratory plastic garlands. Per Nepalese custom, in lieu of the ring exchange, a pinch of red powder was placed on the bride's forehead to demonstrate that she is spoken for. After the ceremony and a few photo ops, the newlyweds were picked up at base camp by helicopter and safely transported home to Katmandu. That they and their surprise nuptials were welcomed by the bride's family was no small feat, either. The sky-high destination of their wedding was not the only unconventional aspect of the union. Nepal is a country that adheres to a firm caste system and arranged marriages.

However, the bride, from the community of Newar, and the groom, a Sherpa, ignored the rules and allowed their love for each other and their enthusiasm for climbing to prevail. They spent their first night as husband and wife in the bride's family's home.

Destination Bride III

Pamela Anderson is a three-time destination-wedding bride. After a four-day courtship, she and rocker Tommy Lee tied the knot in Cancun, Mexico, in 1995. Her second marriage to Kid Rock occurred aboard a yacht in Saint-Tropez in 2006. However, her Vegas marriage to Rick Salomon may have been the quickest of the quickies. The couple slotted it in during her break between the 7:00 PM and 10:00 PM shows of magician Hans Klok's "The Beauty of Magic," in which she performed at the Planet Hollywood Resort & Casino.

Definitely Not All About the Dress

A Valentine's Day weekend wedding in Jamaica…ocean view…sandy beaches…what could be more romantic? Oh, and you'll be tying the knot along with a couple of dozen other naked, sweaty couples. Some weddings are black tie optional; this wedding was clothing optional. The largest documented multicouple nude wedding took place at Superclubs' Hedonism III in Runaway Bay, Jamaica, in February 2003. This was the third annual nude-wedding event for the hotel. What do you expect? The name of the resort is Hedonism, not Wholesome-ism.

Milly: "Well, it wouldn't hurt you to learn some manners, too."

Adam: "What do I need manners for? I already got me a wife."

–Milly Pontipee (Jane Powell) and Adam Pontipee (Howard Keel),
Seven Brides for Seven Brothers (1954)

VIVA LAS VEGAS!

Who among us has not at least wondered, for even a fleeting moment, what it must be like to fly to Vegas and get married amid the whirlwind and hubbub of a city that never sleeps? For decades, Las Vegas has been the destination of choice for engaged couples wanting to add a little celebrity to their wedding service.

Graceland Chapel

If you would like the King himself, or at least, an Elvis Presley impersonator, to walk you down the aisle and maybe even serenade you a little, the best place to host this kind of planned chaos is the Graceland Chapel. Nothing lasts for long in Vegas. So the fact that the Elvis-themed chapel—which heralds itself as the first freestanding wedding chapel in Las Vegas—is still going strong after more than 50 years is a testament to its popularity.

Tantalizing Trivia about Graceland

☞ If you are a first-timer in Las Vegas trying to get to the Graceland Chapel on time, do not fret. The popular wedding destination is located right on the Strip.

☞ Among the many notable celebrities choosing Graceland Chapel to tie the knot is musician Jon Bon Jovi. Jon and Dorothea Hurley, his high school sweetheart, exchanged their wedding vows on April 29, 1989.

☞ Jon returned to the chapel with his band in 2000 to serenade 75 couples who were exchanging their vows during a mass ceremony that day.

☞ Real Elvis aficionados might want to consider getting married at the Chapel in the Woods at Graceland, Elvis' estate. The estate itself was opened for public tours on June 7, 1982, as a museum to the King of Rock'n'Roll. The chapel is literally tucked in the woods behind the estate.

The Little White Wedding Chapel

The pinnacle of convenience, Las Vegas' most famous elopement destination is open 24 hours a day, has an ATM machine right in the lobby and even features a drive-thru marriage service. Sadly, you can't get fries with that, just a little note for the suggestion box.

The chapel is run by ordained minister and "Wedding Queen of the West" Charlotte Richards and offers all the amenities a quickie-wedding couple could desire. Along with the 165-foot (50-meter) Tunnel of Love Drive Thru, the Little White Wedding Chapel offers all the wedding conveniences. You can purchase your gown the day of the wedding at the well-stocked wedding dress store, select flowers from the full floral shop, employ the services of a multilingual translator and webcast the ceremony to friends and family at home, the next-best thing to having them there.

Famous Unions at the Little White Wedding Chapel

Rita Hayworth and Dick Haymes (1953)

Mary Tyler Moore and Richard Meeker (1955)

Frank Sinatra and Mia Farrow (1966)

Patty Duke and Michael Tell (1970)

George Hamilton and Alana Stewart (1972)

Joan Collins and Peter Holm (1985)

Patty Duke (again) and Michael Pearce (1986)

Bruce Willis and Demi Moore (1987)

Stone Cold Steve Austin and Debra Marshall (2000)

Natalie Maines and Adrian Pasdar (2000)

Robert Shapiro and Erika Siebert (2004)

Britney Spears and Jason Alexander (2004)

DID YOU  KNOW?

The Little White Wedding Chapel in fact consists of five chapels: the original Little White Wedding Chapel, Chapel of Promises, Chapel L'Amour, Crystal Chapel and Gazebo, plus, of course, the Tunnel of Love Drive Thru. The original chapel was dubbed the Michael Jordan Chapel after he exchanged vows there with Juanita Vanoy in 1989.

Other Famous Vegas Elopers

All prime examples of what happens in Vegas…is annulled or dissolved soon after.

☛ Carmen Electra and Dennis Rodman at the Little Chapel of the Flowers (1998)

☛ Angelina Jolie (her second marriage) and Billy Bob Thornton (his fifth trip down the aisle) at the Little Church of the West Chapel (2000)

☛ Nicky Hilton (the other Hilton sister) and Todd Andrew Meister at the Las Vegas Wedding Chapel (2004)

Some people claim that marriage interferes with romance. There's no doubt about it. Anytime you have a romance, your wife is bound to interfere.

–Groucho Marx, from *The Groucho Phile* (1976)

WEDDING DISASTERS

At least things can only get better from here!

Murphy's Law

Just because your wedding doesn't go according to plan doesn't mean your marriage is doomed. For proof, look to the nuptials of Bob and Sheri Stritof, coauthors of *The Everything Great Marriage Book*. The banquet hall booked for their reception declared bankruptcy and went out of business one week before the ceremony. Then the priest forgot to come to the rehearsal, all the photographer's equipment was lost or stolen and the bride's special-order gown did not arrive until two hours before the ceremony! Despite a rough beginning, the Stritofs have been happily married for 45 years.

Banquet Bandit

Unforeseen events can put a damper on even the best-planned wedding. Fortunately, one bride and groom did not learn of their misfortune until after they'd returned from their honeymoon. It might be one of the saddest displays of theft on a traditionally happy day since the Grinch dressed up as Santa Claus and stole gifts from the Whos in Whoville. At the Garden Grove, California, wedding of Anthony and Jennifer Smith, an uninvited "guest" walked out of the reception with about $1500 in cash gifts. Video footage revealed an unidentified man snatching envelopes from the gift box in the lobby of the Garden Room banquet facility. Perhaps guests were too busy doing the Chicken Dance to detect the wedding crasher among them. It did not help that he had blended in cunningly well. The fact that he was dressed in the appropriate wedding-party colors of burgundy and blue suggested the theft might have been an inside job. Even though the thief's sticky fingers were caught on tape and subsequently viewed by guests, no one recognized the banquet bandit, and he remained at large.

Buffy, the Hurricane Slayer

Even celebrities have wedding mishaps. Having a heap of money, top-notch wedding planners, and a staff of assistants, personal trainers and hair and make-up people at your disposal doesn't ensure a flawless wedding. Sarah Michelle Gellar and Freddie Prinze Jr., costars of the *Scooby-Doo* movies and *I Know What you Did Last Summer*, might know a thing or two about survival and solving problems and mysteries, but they probably didn't predict that they would have to use their survival skills on their wedding weekend. First, their late-summer 2002 wedding at the El Careyes Beach Resort in Mexico was threatened by Hurricane Hernan. Crazy winds and storms forced the planned outdoor festivities to move inside. The very next day, the area was struck by an earthquake scoring a 4.6 on the Richter scale. Everyone was okay, but the event provided an indisputably rocky start to the marriage. Closing on a happy note, as an anniversary gift five years later, Sarah Michelle made the often celebrity-rebuffed move of legally changing her last name to her husband's. Awww...

DID YOU  KNOW?

Gellar and Prinze's wedding might have been a natural disaster, but it did not cost them much. They negotiated a six-figure deal to give British magazine *Hello!* exclusive photo rights to the wedding. That arrangement presumably bankrolled a good portion of the festivities.

Perseverance to Wed

Sarah Michelle Gellar's *Buffy* costar David Boreanaz had his own rocky wedding. He had planned to marry actress Jaime Bergman in September 2001, but the wedding was postponed after the terrorist attacks on 9/11. Their relatively small, intimate wedding did occur two months later at the Ingleside Inn in Palm Springs. The weather, however, took an ugly turn during the reception and caused a total power outage. The staff kept their cool, utilized a back-up generator and served the guests dinner amid extra candles. A romantic resolution, no "Bones" about it.

Worst. Wedding Crash. Ever.

In Hlabisa, KwaZulu-Natal, two brothers decided to crash a wedding. Hlakkaniphani and Sithembiso Ziqubu were asked to leave the event, but, when they did, angry vigilantes attacked them. One brother was stabbed to death, the other severely injured.

Knocked Up? Almost Knocked OUT!

The one thing they had going for them was timing. Because the recent Writer's Guild strike coincided with *Grey's Anatomy* star Katherine Heigl's wedding to musician Josh Kelly, she had plenty of time off for last-minute planning. But that did not guarantee a smooth wedding. Against the bride's advice, Kelly decided to go skiing two days before the wedding, and it did not take a TV-medical-drama writer to predict what would happen. Evidently, Kelly's skiing skills were very rusty. (Josh, there are easier ways than suicide to escape your imminent wedding.) Although he was not seriously hurt, he suffered quite a fall, which, apparently, left an unsightly mark on his nose. Thankfully, photographers can do wonders with Photoshop.

More drama ensued following the wedding. Kelly lost his spanking-new wedding ring the next day. Again, a Freudian-schooled psychologist might diagnose this "accident" as passive-aggressive resistance to being tied down. Fortunately, some guys at a nearby gas station had a metal detector (who doesn't bring their metal detector when getting gas?), and the ring was located. The topper? When the happy couple arrived at the airport to embark on their Mexican honeymoon, Heigl realized she had forgotten her passport!

"Rule number 76: No excuses. Play like a champion!"

–Jeremy Grey (Vince Vaughn), *Wedding Crashers* (2005)

THEME WEDDINGS

It's your day. So, whether you're a lifelong Trekkie, a White Sox fanatic, a dog lover or have a bizarre obsession with triangles, you have the right to incorporate your favorite theme into your wedding. Express yourself!

Ashlee in Wonderland

How cool would it have been if Jefferson Airplane had performed at the reception? *Alice in Wonderland* was the theme for Ashlee Simpson's wedding with her Fall Out Boy, Pete Wentz.

No Grace Slick belting out "White Rabbit"; the guests probably had to contend with the bride's raspy rendition of "Pieces of Me." Wedding planner Mindy Weiss pulled a white rabbit out of her hat and procured a wedding cake adorned with a teapot, top hat and stopwatch, and there were enough clocks strung from trees to make you think Flavor Flav might jump out at you. Appetizers were served on playing-card trays, and cocktails came in DRINK ME bottles.

The theme was entirely appropriate—the character of Alice also tried to tag along with her overshadowing big sister. Ashlee's attempts at following in sister Jessica's footsteps included a less-successful reality-TV show (*Ashlee*), a mediocre music career, a stab at acting in bad movies (*Undiscovered*, anyone?) and even plastic surgery to aspire to her sister's more-attractive face. Ashlee's wedding also included echoes of Jessica; the elder Simpson sister used the *Alice in Wonderland* theme a few years earlier for her 25th birthday party. The with-child bride did beat her sister to the punch with having a baby, though.

A Different Kind of Diamond on your Wedding Day

On July 8, 2006, Dave Kerpen (an alum of dating reality show *Paradise Hotel*) and Carrie Fisher (not to be mistaken for the writer/actress of the same name, and not one of the women he met on the show) stepped onto the baseball diamond at Keyspan Park in Brooklyn and exchanged their vows. For her, the wedding fulfilled a lifelong dream of marrying her soul mate. For him, a die-hard baseball fan, it fulfilled a lifelong dream of setting foot on a professional baseball field. After the Brooklyn Cyclones completed their game, Kerpen and Fisher stepped onto home plate, as their bridesmaids and groomsmen beamed from the first and third baselines. They were pronounced husband and wife, and the happy couple exited through a tunnel of raised baseball bats held sword-style by the Cyclone players. Then the crowd of 8000 spectators went wild.

They Put the Hearse in Rehearsal Dinner

"I'm not a freak or Satan worshipper or cult member. It just goes with our theme." That was Scott Amsler's defense for why he and then-fiancée Miranda Patterson decided to have their wedding in a cemetery. Indeed, a recurring theme in their relationship has been hearses. Amsler first caught Patterson's attention at a party in November 2005, when he rolled up in a hearse he had refurbished himself. He proposed the following year by attaching an engraved plate reading, "Will you marry me?" to the side of Edgar (the name attributed to his beloved hearse). Sticking with their theme, the couple gained approval from the local cemetery committee to exchange their vows in a gazebo in a three-acre (1-hectare) cemetery in St. Louis.

Cyndie Nunamaker and Brian Wilson go to White Castle

Would you like fries with your wedding? On Valentine's Day, 2008, three couples, including Cyndie Nunamaker and Brian Wilson of Plain City, Ohio, pledged their love for each other—and for those tasty slyders—in a White Castle-themed wedding. The couples were all winners of a local radio contest in the burger joint's founding city of Columbus. The ceremony featured employee nametags worn on the grooms' jackets and a flower girl tossing salt and pepper packets. The *pièce de résistance*? A wedding cake resembling a White Castle tray of burgers, fries and a drink! How's that for a romantic way to celebrate Valentine's Day?

Strange Love: Pirate Marries the Geisha

Sometimes a bride and groom just cannot agree on a theme. When Madame Strange married her magician husband, Sensei Strange (those might not be their real names…just a guess), she looked like she belonged in 17th-century Japan. He looked like he'd just been shipwrecked while searching for buried treasure with One-Eyed Willie. The geisha-bride idea was sparked when the Strange pair were living together in Japan. The Sensei bought his love an antique wedding kimono, and, when he later proposed, she knew she would wear it, along with full porcelain make-up and black wig, for the wedding. He, meanwhile, wanted to emulate Jack Sparrow—or, at least, the delusional pirate guy from *Dodgeball*. The pair decided to go all out, Crouching Tiger, Hidden Treasure style. The pagan ceremony was held in October 2006—appropriately, just three days before Halloween, so guests were encouraged to get in on the dress-up fun. Everything seemed to go off without a hitch, until the inevitable question arose as to whether there were any objectors to the marriage. Another "pirate" dramatically stood up and was subsequently "shot down" by the pistol-wielding swashbuckler of a groom. And with that, the couple vowed to spend the rest of their Strange days together. Till death do they pa-arghhh-rt.

A Wedding Carol

They met in the theater: he was in the chorus, she was the lead in their local production of *Funny Girl*. Chris Bowlsby and Windy Merrill felt it only natural that their wedding reflect how they met and their love of theater. Deciding on a classic Dickens holiday theme, the pair chose for the ceremony the old-fashioned Heights Theater in Columbia Heights, Minnesota, and called the blessed event "One Wedding and No Funeral." As guests arrived, ushers dressed in red jackets, hats and white gloves escorted them to their seats with flashlights. The bride and her female costars wore Victorian garb and hats; the men dressed in black frock coats with cream gloves and gold vests. After the ceremony, the bride and groom promenaded down the aisle to the theme from *The Muppet Show*. Onward, to the reception, held at the McNamara Alumni Center, where guests mingled during a montage of scenes from Chris and Windy's favorite films and sat at movie-themed tables, each sporting a movie-reel centerpiece adorned with fresh flowers. When it was time for the final credits to roll, the couple made their exit amid a flurry of popcorn tossed by guests. And they lived happily ever after. The End.

Jane: "*Theme wedding!*"

Kevin: "*What was the theme? Humiliation?*"

–Jane Nichols (Katherine Heigl) and Kevin Doyle (James Marsden),
27 Dresses (2008)

PARANORMAL WEDDINGS

So you say you don't believe in ghosts? Then try and explain away these otherworldly wedding tales. You might find yourself having a change of heart.

Remember Me

In 2001, the *St. Paul Pioneer Press* ran a rather unusual article highlighting part of Kimberly and Joseph Arrigoni's wedding day. By all accounts, the event, held in March of that year, was a joyous one—family and friends enjoyed a beautiful service in a perfect setting. The Landmark Center in St. Paul, Minnesota, where the wedding was held, is a cultural hub in the midst of a modern city. But even more amazing is the building itself. Erected in 1902, the Landmark Center was once a Federal Court House and post office.

Over the years, the building fell into disrepair and was in danger of being demolished, until a group of conservation-minded residents restored it to its original glory. A five-story courtyard, 20-foot (6-meter) ceilings, all the marble and mahogany touches you can imagine and turrets and spires that put you in mind of medieval England made this nationally recognized historic place the perfect venue for the Arrigoni's wedding—and a perfect setting for wedding photos. At one point, the bridal party gathered on the stairway near the second-floor balcony for a photo. When the couple received the photos back a couple of months later, something seemed a little off with that particular picture. Blurred in the background, standing behind the five-year-old ring bearer, was the faded image of a ruddy-looking fellow. Nobody knew who he was—or what he was.

After a little investigative work, the Arrigonis learned that the ghost of legendary gangster Jack Peifer haunted the Landmark Center, and that their picture was—as the *St. Paul Pioneer Press* put it—the "first photographic evidence" of the fact. Peifer was once a middleman in the Barker-Karpis gang during America's Prohibition era and was found guilty in that very building when it operated as a courthouse. When he heard he would be spending the next 30 years in Leavenworth Prison, Peifer killed himself by swallowing potassium cyanide. Not a nice death—or a nice story. But staff who've reported feeling Peifer's presence say the convict isn't a threatening ghost. And, if the Arrigonis' photo is any indication, perhaps the old guy is just a little lonely.

Good or Evil?

Given the chance, most of us would choose good over evil. But, sometimes, it takes an extraordinary event to make us recognize the harsh realities of the destructive path we are on. For Colorado resident Joe Martinez, a chance perusal through an old photo album shocked him into understanding just how damning his ongoing battle with drug use was to his life.

In October 2007, Joe and his wife, Patty, were scanning through pictures of his in-laws' 50th-anniversary celebration, which had taken place eight years earlier. One photo, in particular, caught the couple's attention. It was a photograph of the two of them, standing before the celebratory head table, and, although there was not another person in the frame, they were far from alone. Peering over Joe's left shoulder was what the couple described as a "devil dog," with large, piercing eyes, prominent dark coloring and a mouth full of teeth. It was a concrete sign of what the couple had known for many years— that Joe was struggling with demons in his life.

"I thought, man, you're really walking with Satan," Patty told news reporters as the couple shared their story.

The picture was examined by photo experts, who all agreed that it did not appear to bear any sign of tampering. It was not a double exposure, and, although other family members also snapped the same picture, the demon dog did not appear in any of their photos. For Joe, the photograph made a statement—he needed to make some choices in his life.

"There's good and evil in life. There's the good on the right side," Joe told FOX News reporters, nodding to his wife. "And there's the evil on the left-hand side."

Since their discovery, Joe has carried the photo around with him at all times, often tucking it into his Bible or wallet. The couple credits the discovery for helping Joe kick his drug habit.

Urban Legend or Ghostly Encounter?

One Chinese legend tells of an old carpenter named Wang, who had no end of commissions for his work. One night, after working particularly late, Wang left his studio to make his way home. Tired and moving along on automatic pilot, Wang found himself walking in a particularly remote area with nary a house in sight. He decided to ask at the first house he came across if he could rest there for the night, and, soon enough, he noticed a light flickering in a distant window. A scary-looking fellow, haggard and old, with chiseled features and green eyes, answered his knock. Although a little unnerved by the sight of the man standing before him, Wang nonetheless asked if he could stay the night, explaining that he was lost. After a moment or two of thought, the old man agreed. When Wang entered the house, he noticed a beautiful but clearly distraught young girl. Wang asked the man if this was his daughter. The man replied, quite hastily, that he was marrying the young girl. He then instructed Wang to go to sleep and leave at dawn. Wang was only too happy to oblige the man and left the next morning, without even bidding his host goodbye.

Wang hadn't traveled far, however, before he realized that he'd left his hat behind. When he retraced his steps, he found only a few graves and his hat, sitting atop one of them, where the house should have been. To say he was frightened is an understatement. He was not, however, frightened enough to forego asking a few questions on his way back home. What he learned sent even more shivers down his spine. According to the legend, the man he'd visited was in fact deceased, and the young girl he'd seen was a ghost. Apparently, the old man's children had not wanted their father to walk through the afterlife alone, so they arranged for the girl to be buried beside him.

Getting Wed When You're Dead

The Chinese have an interesting practice called "ghost marriage." If you think this means that the bride and groom are dead, you are absolutely correct! The Chinese use ghost marriage for a number of reasons: to unite two deceased people who were engaged during their lifetime, to continue the family name, and to marry off an unmarried daughter. Historians are not exactly sure how the practice of ghost marriage originated, but these ceremonies are still being conducted to this day, and they are not solely a Chinese practice. Variations of ghost marriage are known to have occurred around the world, from Africa to India and even in post–World War I France.

Ghostly Guests

When you think about it, it's probably impossible to contain a ghost. If centuries of perception are in any way accurate, ghosts are a little transparent. And they can walk through walls. So it might boggle the mind, just a little, to learn about one wedding venue that caters to newlyweds and the deceased, all at the same time.

Back in 1936, a ship named the *Queen Mary*, built by the Cunard Line of the United Kingdom, set sail on its first journey. A luxury cruise liner, the *Queen Mary* started her life at sea as a passenger ship, but, from 1940 to 1946, during World War II, she served as a military vessel. After the war, she returned to her first incarnation as a passenger ship and continued in that capacity until she was retired to California's Long Beach shipyards in 1967.

It was just a matter of time before the once-glorious ship was reinvented as a museum of the sea, a place to dine on elegant cuisine and a venue for special events. However, before long, the *Queen Mary* started to gain a reputation for having a few permanent guests of the deceased kind on board; reports of ghosts wandering the ship were not uncommon. The stories so captivated the imagination of visitors (many of whom experienced these ghostly entities firsthand) that two types of paranormal tours were set up—an ordinary tour and a hunt, in which visitors can actually witness a ghost hunter's "tools of the trade." In the meantime, it has become rather fashionable to host wedding receptions in the ship's historic ballroom. Not only do guests experience an amazing setting and great food, they might find themselves visiting with a wedding crasher from another era!

Spice Up Your Romance!

Thayer's Hotel in Annandale, Minnesota, is a destination favorite for wedding planners. Gus Thayer and his wife, Caroline, built the three-story Victorian hotel in 1895, shortly after the couple moved to Annandale. Over the last century, the Thayer Hotel has gained a reputation for being haunted, and it is a reputation that current owner Sharon Gammell celebrates. Not only are visitors welcome to participate in anything from murder mystery dinners to ghost-hunting classes, Thayer's Historic Bed 'n' Breakfast hosts weddings with as many as 50 persons any day of the year. If you are interested in a package deal, Sharon will even officiate the ceremony. Just remember to plan for a few extra guests: the Thayers, along with an assortment of long-deceased visitors, have been known to stop by on a regular basis. And they are not shy about making their presence known, even in the middle of a wedding ceremony. During one ceremony, Sharon, who was officiating, asked who was giving away the bride. Sadly, the bride's father was deceased, but, just as Sharon asked the question, the bride felt a ghostly kiss on her cheek.

"One of the wedding guests happened to take a photo at the same time, and there is clearly an 'orb' on the bride's cheek!" says Sharon. "The guest took another [photo] a minute later, and the 'orb' was gone."

The Thayer Hotel is listed on the National Registry of Historic Places and has been named a Property of the Year by the Minnesota Association of Innkeepers. It is also listed as one of the "Top 10 Best Haunted Places to Stay" in the United States—all pretty good reasons to say your "I do's" at this unique location.

> *"Isn't the view beautiful? It takes my breath away. Well, it would if I had any."*
>
> –Corpse Bride (Helena Bonham Carter), *The Corpse Bride* (2005)

THE HONEYMOON

Today's average honeymoon lasts nine days and costs about $4000. Hawaii is the most popular honeymoon destination for American couples, visited by about a third of all newlyweds, and the Caribbean is a close second. Niagara Falls, the most popular honeymoon spot half a century ago, is not even in the top five today. And long before Niagara Falls was in vogue, honeymoons were quite different.

Happy Hideaway

The modern idea of flying off to some exotic location and enjoying a honeymoon with your new spouse is just that, modern. Originally, the honeymoon—or *hjunottsmanathr*, to use the Norse term—was anything but a happy event. The term has its roots in early Northern European history and stems from a time when brides were kidnapped from neighboring villages. The bride's family, displeased by the abduction, organized a search party, so the groom took his new wife into hiding until her family gave up the search. Hence, the meaning behind the word honeymoon: hiding.

Celebrity Honeymoon Locations

☛ John F. Kennedy and Jacqueline Bouvier (1953): Acapulco, Mexico, and then onto the San Ysidro Ranch in Montecito, California

☛ Marilyn Monroe and Joe DiMaggio (1954): Japan, with Monroe sneaking away to Korea for four days to perform for U.S. troops

☛ Elvis and Priscilla Presley (1967): Palm Springs, California

☛ Prince Charles and Princess Diana (1981): aboard the royal yacht *Britannia*, cruising the Mediterranean Sea

☛ Woody Allen and Soon-Yi Previn (1997): Paris, France

☛ Barbra Streisand and James Brolin (1998): Barbados

☛ Michael Douglas and Catherine Zeta-Jones (2000): their Aspen, Colorado, home

☛ Nicole Kidman and Keith Urban (2006): the 13,000-square-foot (1200-square-meter) private Royal Estate at the St. Regis in Bora Bora

☛ Eva Longoria and Tony Parker (2007): Parrot Cay in the Turks and Caicos

☛ Pete Wentz and Ashlee Simpson (2008): Caribbean

☛ Jenna Bush and Henry Hager (2008): Lanai, Hawaii

Don't Faux Pas in Fiji

An up-and-coming honeymoon hotspot, if you can afford it, is Fiji. However, Fijians have their own unique etiquette, which tourists visiting a traditional village are advised to adhere to, according to honeymoon travel website thebigday.com.

☛ Don't wear a hat. This is considered insulting to the chief.

☛ Don't bring alcohol. It is banned from many villages.

☛ Don't touch someone's head or wear shoes into people's houses; it is disrespectful.

☛ Don't wear shorts. Women should avoid bare shoulders or exposed midriffs.

☛ Don't take advantage of hospitality or abuse kindness. In their culture, Fijians are expected to offer visitors meals, their time or a place to stay…even if they cannot afford it.

☛ Do offer your host a gift, food or money in exchange for a hosted meal or overnight stay.

☛ Do dress modestly. A sulu makes an excellent cover-up.

☛ Do speak calmly and quietly. Loud voices are interpreted as anger.

☛ Do bring a gift of kava root to show your respect. A pound (454 grams) is sufficient.

☛ Don't lavish too much praise on an item; the Fijians will feel compelled to offer it as a gift.

DID YOU  **KNOW?**

Richard Huloet's *Abecedarium Anglico Latinum* contained the first written reference to a honeymoon in 1552. It claimed that a honeymoon "was a sardonic reference to the inevitable waning of love like a phase of the moon."

Puts the Honey in Honeymoon

Another interpretation of the origins of the word "honeymoon" comes from an ancient tradition in which the newly married couple drinks a cup of mead daily for their first month of marriage. Mead, in case you are not aware, is made from honey, and the practice of providing enough mead for a month was thought to ensure a happy marriage with lots of children.

DID YOU  **KNOW?**

There are at least three horror flicks in which the honeymoon is somehow featured: *The Honeymoon Killers* (1970), *Zombie Honeymoon* (2004) and *Dark Honeymoon* (2007). If you're into thrillers, they aim to please. Problem is, you likely shouldn't watch them when you're actually on your honeymoon.

You know the honeymoon is pretty much over when you start to go out with the boys on Wednesday nights, and so does she.

–unknown

GROWING OLD TOGETHER

A wedding in and of itself can be epic. But it is also only the beginning.

Pearls of Wisdom

Every year, the Middlebrook Farms assisted-living facility in Trumbull, Connecticut, invites a member of the clergy to preside over a wedding vow renewal ceremony for its residents and their spouses. Streamers, balloons and even a wedding cake heighten the event. In June 2008, 12 elderly couples walked (or used a walker or were wheeled) down the aisle to reaffirm their love. They renewed their vows and had their rings blessed. What advice do these pros have for young couples hoping to cultivate a lasting partnership?

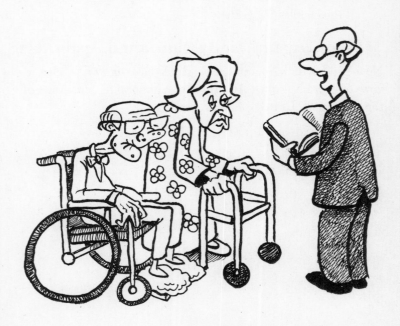

☛ "Just keep your mouth shut." –Frank Detwiler, 78, who attended the celebration to honor 51 years of marriage to his wife, Phyllis, 75.

☛ "Tolerance. [And]…we don't talk at the same time." –Ruth Wilson, 78, who celebrated 57 years of marriage to her high school sweetheart, Warren.

☛ "Not to antagonize each other. Sometimes it's impossible, but try it." –Betty Salamon, who renewed her vows to husband, Matt, after 60 years of marriage.

☛ "Listen to your wife." –John Stephen, 92, who experienced a second chance at love with wife Frances, 91, after both of their respective spouses passed away. They renewed their vows after 20 years together.

☛ "Let him do as he pleases." –Veronica Ruth Schreyer, who, along with husband George, boasted the longest marriage of all the couples: 72 years!

I Do…Again…and Again…and Again…

New Yorkers Richard and Carole Roble have renewed their vows a record 55 times! And they have done so in every state in the contiguous United States of America.

Long-standing and Long-living

In a report dated Sunday, June 26, 2005, from India's national daily newspaper, *The Hindu*, comes a story of record-breaking wedded bliss. The story introduced Philipose Thomas and his wife, Sosamma. The couple, who, by that point, had managed to celebrate a staggering 86 anniversaries together, were married on February 17, 1918, in a Christian ceremony held at St. Simon's Jacobite Syrian Church, located in the Central Travancore region of Kerala. Philipose was just 13 years old at the time of the arranged marriage and his blushing bride only 12. Still, their marriage has weathered the years and produced seven children, although their first child was not born until they had been married for 15 years.

Likewise, Temulji Nariman and Lady Nariman were only five years old when they wed, but the duo also went on to celebrate 86 wedding anniversaries. Is there even a traditional anniversary gift for these milestones?

Anniversary Gifts

The traditional first anniversary gift is paper, so consider a book of poetry, a wedding scrapbook or tickets to the ballet (for her) or an NBA game (for him). The second anniversary traditionally dictates a cotton gift. Options include new bedding, a new dress (for her) or suit (for him). The third is leather. Whips and chains? (Kidding!) How about a leather wallet, a bomber jacket or a nice belt? The fourth calls for fruit and/or flowers. Consider planting a rose bush; if your anniversary happens to fall during blooming season, plant early and let your spouse enjoy the nice surprise. Alternatively, a nice fruit basket with a sweet card might be sufficient. For your fifth anniversary, wood is called for. How about a piece of furniture or a wood-framed photograph?

Other Traditional Anniversary Gifts

Sixth: Candy/Iron

Seventh: Wool/Copper

Eighth: Bronze/Pottery

Ninth: Pottery (Does Pottery Barn count?)

Tenth: Tin/Aluminum

Eleventh: Steel

Twelfth: Silk/Linen

Thirteenth: Lace

Fourteenth: Ivory

Fifteenth: Crystal

Twentieth: China

Twenty-fifth: Silver

Thirtieth: Pearls

Thirty-fifth: Coral

Fortieth: Ruby

Forty-fifth: Sapphire

Fiftieth: Gold

Fifty-fifth: Emerald

Sixtieth: Diamond

Modern Anniversary Gifts

Some consider the traditional anniversary gifts outdated or unromantic. Who really procures genuine ivory anymore? And aren't appliances more practical than fruit or flowers? Following are the more recent anniversary gift suggestions, with some slight variances from the traditional:

First: Clocks

Second: China (perhaps piece-set what you didn't get from your registry)

Third: Crystal/Glass (ditto above)

Fourth: Appliances

Fifth: Silverware

Sixth: Candy/Iron

Seventh: Desk Sets

Eighth: Bronze/Pottery

Ninth: Linen/Lace

Tenth: Leather

Eleventh: Jewelry

Twelfth: Pearls

Thirteenth: Textiles/Furs

Fourteenth: Gold Jewelry

Fifteenth: Watches

Twentieth: Platinum

Twenty-fifth: Silver

Thirtieth: Diamond

Thirty-fifth: Jade

Fortieth: Ruby

Forty-fifth: Sapphire

Fiftieth: Gold

Fifty-fifth: Emerald

Sixtieth: Diamond

For two people in a marriage to live together day after day is unquestionably the one miracle the Vatican has overlooked.

–Bill Cosby, American actor and comedian

ABOUT THE ILLUSTRATOR

Roger Garcia

Roger Garcia is a self-taught artist with some formal training who specializes in cartooning and illustration. He is an immigrant from El Salvador, and during the last few years, his work has been primarily cartoons and editorial illustrations in pen and ink. Recently, he has started painting once more. Focusing on simplifying the human form, he uses a bright minimal palette and as few elements as possible. His work can be seen in newspapers, magazines, promo material and on www.rogergarcia.ca.

ABOUT THE AUTHORS

Rachel Conard

Born and raised in Racine, Rachel Conard has been writing all her life. Her first grade teacher would let the other students "check out" her stories as if they were part of the library. And when she accompanied her father on fishing trips up north, she was more concerned about keeping her notebook dry than reeling in the 10-pound musky her dad had caught. A graduate in journalism from the University of Wisconsin-Milwaukee, Rachel loves spending time with family and friends, eating good food, enjoying a smart cocktail and playing a few party games. Her previous work has been published in the *Milwaukee Shepherd Express*, and she cowrote *The Bathroom Book of Wisconsin Trivia*.

Lisa Wojna

Lisa is the coauthor of more than a dozen trivia books and the sole author of nine other nonfiction books. She has worked in the community newspaper industry as a writer and journalist and has traveled all over the world. Although writing and photography have been a central part of her life for as long as she can remember, it's the people behind every story that are her motivation and give her the most fulfilment.